THE ULTIMATE HISTORY OF
BMW

This is a Parragon Publishing book

This edition published in 2005

Parragon Publishing
Queen Street House
4 Queen Street
Bath BA1 1HE, UK

A copy of the CIP data for this book is available from the British Library upon request.

The rights of Andrew Noakes to be identified as the author of this work have been asserted in accordance with Section 77 of the Copyright, Designs and Patents Act of 1988.

Created, designed, produced and packaged by Stonecastle Graphics Ltd

Designed by Sue Pressley and Paul Turner
Edited by Philip de Ste. Croix

Printed and bound in Indonesia

The author and publishers have made every reasonable effort to contact all copyright holders. Any errors that may have occurred are inadvertent and anyone who for any reason has not been contacted is invited to write to the publishers so that a full acknowledgement may be made in subsequent editions of this work.

ISBN: 1-40545-316-8

Photographic credits:

Reinhard Lintelmann: Pages 48, 49, 57(b), 62, 64(br), 68, 71.

Photographs © Neill Bruce's Automobile Photolibrary, by Neill Bruce and others: Pages 17(tr), 17(br), 21(b), 24, 27(b), 28, 29, 30, 31, 32(t), 32(bl), 33, 34(br), 36(tr), 36(c), 43, 45, 52, 53, 57(t), 64(bl), 65, 66(tl), 73(tl), 74(l), 75(bl), 75(br), 86-87, 94-95, 106(l), 107, 109(tl), 109(bl), 117, 121(t), 123(tr), 136, 139(tr), 139(cr), 141, 143(t), 144, 145(b), 146-7, 151, 156, 160, 161, 162.
Toni Bader: Page 152.
Stefan Donat: Page 131.
Geoffrey Goddard: Pages 17(tl), 20(bl), 32(br), 34(tr), 34(bl), 35(b), 108,
Christof Gonzenbach: Pages 37, 176, 177(t), 178(b).
David Hodges: Page 134(tl).
Stefan Lüscher: Pages 164, 165(b), 170, 181.
Richard Meinert: Page 169(t).
F. Naaf: Page 159(r).
Jörg Petersen: Page 179.

All other photographs are from the BMW Heritage Archive, with many thanks.

THE ULTIMATE HISTORY OF
BMW

ANDREW NOAKES

p

Above: The Z4 blends eye-catching looks with accomplished handling and exceptional straight-line speed.

CONTENTS

Above: The 328 was the ultimate BMW of the pre-war years. Its influence would continue to be felt well into the 1950s.

INTRODUCTION

Today's desirable, technically advanced BMW cars do not even hint at the first vehicles the company made, nearly 80 years ago. They were as small and humble as anything on the road, at first no more than license-built British Austin Sevens assembled at Eisenach, in the center of Germany. BMW quickly refined that basic machine and then replaced it with a car of its own design. Since then there has rarely been a BMW which has attracted anything but praise for its engineering, and anything but respect and admiration for its technical achievements.

BMW really arrived with the innovative 328 sports car of the 1930s, which made a huge impact in Europe and in Britain and continued to exert an influence on car design long after the war. By then BMW was virtually in ruins, its car manufacturing plant lost to the Soviet-controlled zone of East Germany, and its activities curtailed under post-war rules which prevented it from building even big motorcycles, let alone cars. When car production did finally start again in 1951, BMW embarked on a disastrous policy chasing a market for expensive, high-quality cars – but in post-war Germany that market was tiny, and already dominated by the might of Mercedes-Benz. In the wake of the 1956 Suez crisis BMW built its own version of the ultra-economical Isetta bubble car, but the end of the bubble car boom left BMW saddled with an old-fashioned range that was ill-equipped to match the market conditions it faced. By the end of the 1950s BMW faced takeover by arch-rival Mercedes-Benz, and oblivion.

The company's luck changed in the 1960s with the launch of an attractive range of 'Neue Klasse' cars boasting compact dimensions, attractive styling and swift performance. Big sellers, they set up BMW's renaissance, which continued into the 1970s with a well-structured range of cars starting in 1972 with the 5-series cars built at a new factory in Dingolfing. The smaller 3-series and larger 7-series arrived later in the 1970s along with a 6-series coupé line which took over from the CS coupés which had done so much to further BMW's reputation both on the road and in European Touring Car racing. BMW diversified in the 1980s, building a range of high-performance cars underpinned by a championship-winning Formula 1 effort, but also extending its range of road cars to include capacious station wagons, all-season four-wheel-drive sedans, and advanced diesels. And it built the 627bhp engine that powered the McLaren F1, the fastest road car ever made. BMW underlined its engineering expertise with wins at Le Mans and a return to F1 with the most powerful engines in the sport. And it looked to the future by developing advanced concept cars powered by electricity and by hydrogen.

The story which unfolds in the pages that follow is one of unparalleled achievement in the design of aero engines, motorcycles and especially cars, but also one which has sometimes teetered perilously close to the edge of disaster. Today BMW is stronger and more widely respected than ever, and the story isn't over yet.

THE BIRTH
OF BMW
1916-30

Above: BMW's famous blue and white logo is a graphically stylized version of a spinning aircraft propeller.

Previous pages: Dixis take pride of place in BMW's Berlin showroom in 1929.

Right: The Eisenach factory, which BMW acquired in 1928, started by building cars like this Wartburg in 1898. Both gasoline and electric cars were produced in the early days.

THOUGH IT is such a familiar badge today sported by BMW motor cars and motorcycles around the world, the company's blue and white roundel recalls an era when BMW operated in a very different technical arena. The badge is a stylized version of a spinning airplane propeller in a blue sky – or, depending on which story you believe, in the blue and white colors of Bavaria, the southern German state where BMW was founded. The colors may be incidental, but the shape is fundamental: BMW's origins lie not in the manufacture of motor cars, nor even motorcycles, but in the rapidly-expanding aircraft industry of the early 1900s.

German engineer Nikolaus Otto's company Gasmotorenfabrik Deutz had produced the first workable internal combustion engines in Cologne in the 1870s, under the technical stewardship of Gottlieb Daimler and Wilhelm Maybach. By the turn of the century the partnership of Daimler and Maybach had been responsible for some of the most advanced motor car designs yet seen, while the internal combustion engine was about to reach for the skies in the hands of the Wright brothers' pioneering aircraft. Within a few years of the Wright brothers' first flight in 1903, aircraft industries were being established across the world. In March 1911 Otto's son, Gustav, began building small aircraft of his own at the Otto Flugmaschinenfabrik (aircraft factory) on the edge of the Oberwiesenfeld airfield, just outside Munich in the south of Germany. Otto's aircraft were successful, and the outbreak of war in 1914, and the increase in aircraft production that resulted from it, further contributed to the company's growing stature within the German aircraft industry. By 1916 Otto's company had been renamed the Bayerische Flugzeug Werke (Bavarian Aircraft Works), and it continued to flourish.

By then a new aero-engine company had set up shop at Oberwiesenfeld, in a factory previously occupied by an aircraft manufacturer called Flugwerke Deutschland. Aircraft engineer Karl Friedrich Rapp established the Rapp Motoren Werke (engine works) with a view to building high performance marine and aero-engines, concentrating on high profile

engines for record attempts. When the war intervened the Rapp company quickly switched to building engines for military aircraft produced at the Otto factory, and ambitious expansion plans were put in place. But it was too much, too soon. When Rapp engines developed a reputation for vibration and fragility, the Rapp factory's prospects suddenly looked grim.

But there was a savior, in the shape of Viennese financier Camillo Castiglioni, who (amongst other things) was a member of the board of Austro-Daimler – originally the Austrian offshoot of the German Daimler company, but a separate entity since 1906. Austro-Daimler had developed a reliable, powerful V12 aero-engine which was now in great demand for the war effort. Its production lines in Vienna were at full stretch, so Castiglioni brokered a deal for Rapp to build more than 200 of the 350hp Austro-Daimler engines under license at his Munich factory. In return Castiglioni effectively took control of the Rapp company, and in July 1917 it was renamed the Bayerische Motoren Werke (Bavarian Engine Works), or BMW.

By then Rapp himself was gone, and the engineering direction of the new company lay in the hands of two newcomers, Franz Josef Popp and Max Friz. Popp had trained as an engineer at Brno in what is now the Czech Republic, and had been sent to Germany by AEG-Union to learn about aircraft engine manufacture. When the deal was done for BMW to manufacture Austro-Daimler aero-engines, Popp was installed in Munich to oversee production. He quickly took over as the factory's general manager, making sweeping changes which included strengthening BMW's engineering team. Popp brought in 33-year-old Max Friz, who had left Daimler after working on such projects as the 1914 Mercedes Grand Prix cars which had finished 1-2-3 in the French Grand Prix. And Friz had a passion for aero-engines.

In complete contrast to Rapp's dubious early efforts the first BMW aero-engine designed under Friz was extraordinarily successful. Called the Type IIIa because of a German government classification system for aero-engines, 'III' being its capacity class, it was an in-line six-cylinder engine – a configuration which BMW would return to again and again in future years – which won many friends thanks to its excellent performance at high altitudes.

Above: The 1899 Decauville was an advanced air-cooled car with independent front suspension. They were built under license at Eisenach.

Above: One of two four-cylinder cars introduced by Dixi in 1904, the S12 helped improve Eisenach's sales.

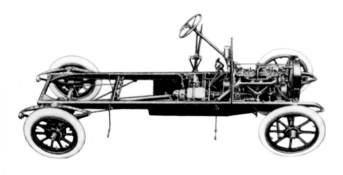

Above: The Dixi S12 chassis, showing the ladder frame and leaf springs that were conventional at the time.

Opposite: Dixi's high prices hampered sales of its smaller cars more than those of bigger machines like this S16.

Some rival engines used superchargers to ensure that the engine ingested sufficient air in the rarefied high-altitude atmosphere, but Friz instead gave the Type IIIa a high compression ratio to ensure that combustion efficiency was high and also to avoid the extra mechanical losses associated with a 'blower.' The drawback of that high compression ratio was the possibility of engine damage cause by 'pinking' or engine knock when the engine was running in the thicker atmosphere near the ground. Friz avoided that by incorporating a two-stage throttle system to ensure that the throttle was only opened fully when the aircraft was at altitude. A special altitude-compensating carburetor further improved high-altitude performance, making the Type IIIa the engine of choice for pilots of Germany's most feared fighter plane of the World War I, the Fokker D.VIIF.

Aero-engines outlawed

But the end of the war brought Germany's aircraft industry back to earth, and BMW with it. The Treaty of Versailles sought to prevent Germany from re-arming, and as a result the production of aircraft and aero-engines was outlawed: German aircraft factories were forced to find alternative work. So even though Franz Zeno Diemer set a new world altitude record of 32,020ft (9760m) using the huge Type IV BMW engine, BMW had to look beyond aero-engines for its income, making ends meet with whatever engineering work it could find. One experiment was with a powered two-wheeler fitted with a 148cc two-stroke engine and called the Flink, but sadly this motorized bicycle was rather heavy and so it did little to live up to its name, which means 'speedy.' Very few were made.

To keep the Munich factory busy BMW made farm equipment and household items, and then secured a major contract to build 10,000 railroad braking systems for Georg Knorr's Berlin-based brake company Knorr-Bremse. This put the Munich company on a firmer footing. Castiglioni took the opportunity to sell his stake in BMW to Knorr-Bremse, but before long he was back with a plan to use BMW's considerable engineering skills on something more exciting than railroad brakes. Castiglioni bought the BMW name back from Knorr-Bremse (which continues to be a major producer of air brake systems for trains and road vehicles today) and set up shop at the now-disused site which had been home to the Bayerische Flugzeug Werke. By now BMW had adopted the famous propeller badge, and the company busied itself building engines for buses, trucks, and stationary applications (powering pumps, generators, and farm equipment). It was for stationary use that Max Friz and Martin Stolle originally designed a 500cc engine with two horizontally-opposed cylinders, this so-called 'boxer' configuration offering excellent balance and freedom from vibration without the expense of a multi-cylinder layout. In addition to its stationary applications, this 'Bayern Kleinmotor' (Bavarian small engine) went into the Victoria motorcycle built at Nuremburg, a couple of hundred miles to the north of Munich, and it also powered the Helios motorcycle built by what was left of the Bayerische Flugzeug Werke. There was some disquiet at BMW about the quality of the two-wheelers now emerging with BMW engines in their frames, but in 1923 Friz was asked to lay out a design for BMW's own motorcycle, and in less than five weeks he had created the first of a long line, the R32.

Throughout the period following the end of the World War I, BMW's engineers had been experimenting not just with powered two-wheelers, but also with four-wheel vehicles. Documents in the company's archive today refer to a prototype four-wheeled vehicle of 1918,

Above: The BMW 'boxer' engine was used for powering pumps and generators before it appeared in motorcycles in the 1920s.

Below right: This 1921 Victoria was one of the first two-wheelers powered by a BMW engine.

Below: BMW created its own motorcycle, the R32, in 1923.

though few details remain about what sort of vehicle it was. Some sources point to BMW involvement with the flat-twin-powered prototype built by Professor Wunibald Kamm. The subject came up again in 1926 when Max Friz and Gotthilf Dürrwächter started planning a range of BMW cars with four- and eight-cylinder engines, but the cars never reached production even though several prototypes were built. Instead BMW moved into motor car production by flexing its new-found financial muscle in 1928, taking over a small car factory in Eisenach, some way to the north of Munich in the center of Germany.

Eisenach's early cars

Fahrzeugfabrik Eisenach was established by Heinrich Ehrhardt in 1896, and the factory started by building all kinds of vehicles – from pedal cycles to gun carriages. Eisenach started making cars two years later, selling light electric vehicles and gasoline-engined machines with Benz engines under the names of Eisenach and Wartburg. Ehrhardt then signed a contract with the French company Decauville, a railroad locomotive manufacturer which had diversified into motor cars, to build its 3.5hp Voiturelle at the Eisenach works. The Decauville was an advanced car with an air-cooled vertical twin engine and independent sliding pillar front suspension – a first for a production car. The French machine would also catch the eye of no less an engineer than Henry Royce, who had one shipped to his Manchester works in 1903. Royce then proceeded to re-engineer the whole car as the basis for the machines that he would sell with the Hon. C.S. Rolls as the Rolls-Royce.

Ehrhardt parted company with the Eisenach firm in 1903, taking his Decauville license with him to a new factory in Dusseldorf. Eisenach regrouped with new models of its own design under the name Dixi, Latin for 'I have spoken,' which was intended to signify that they were the 'last word' in motor cars. So these first Dixi models were impeccably built from the best materials available, and they were put on sale at a premium price. As a result of the high prices Eisenach charged, it was inevitable that sales of the original two-cylinder,

Left: Early BMW motorcycles proved successful in competition. Ernest Henne, later a BMW racing driver, won the 1926 Wildpark Karlsruhe race on a racing R47.

shaft-drive S6 and single-cylinder, chain-drive T7 models were slow, though the four-cylinder S10 and S12 models which followed in 1904 found customers in greater numbers. Even bigger sales were in store for the mid-range 14PS R8 (available as a four-seat tourer or a popular two-seater sporting model) and the big 32PS S16. The Dixi factory also produced adaptations of these designs to turn them into commercial units and special-purpose vehicles, such as ambulances.

Eisenach's workshops were just getting properly into their stride when war intervened in 1914, and the factory was turned over to military production. Car manufacture did not restart at Eisenach until 1919 and it was another two years before new post-war Dixi designs appeared, in the form of the imposing (and expensive) four-cylinder G1. But the G1 was the wrong car for the times: in the depressed post-war years few Germans could afford new cars, and those who could were increasingly looking to imported American machines. German companies found that there were few export opportunities for a vanquished foe. It was a story which presaged the fortunes of BMW in the years following World War II, as the company proferred unsuitable products to an unreceptive market. The effect was the same as it would be 40 years later – the company rapidly headed towards bankruptcy.

What Eisenach clearly needed was a reasonably-priced small car more in tune with the austerity market of the post-war years. Developing a new model to do that job would have been time-consuming and expensive, so instead the cash-strapped company applied the same principle that Ehrhardt had used at the turn of the century: it looked abroad to find a suitable machine that could be built at Eisenach under license. It found exactly what it was looking for in the British Austin Seven.

BMW Dixi 3/15 DA-1

Production	1928-29
Engine	In-line four-cylinder, eight side valves, cast iron cylinder block and head
Bore x stroke	56mm x 76.2mm
Capacity	747cc
Power	10.5bhp at 2400rpm
Torque	Not quoted
Fuel system	Single updraft carburetor
Gearbox	Three-speed manual, single dry-plate clutch
Chassis/body	Steel channel-section chassis with separate steel body
Suspension	Front: rigid front axle with radius arms and transverse leaf spring
	Rear: live axle with cantilever leaf springs
Brakes	Drums all round
Performance	Top speed: approximately 40mph (64km/h)

Right: Before the appearance of the Dixi 3/15 DA-1, Eisenach had produced quality cars which sold at a high price. This was a car for the masses.

Dixi's Seven

Herbert Austin designed the Seven himself, laying out the scale drawings on the billiard table at his home with the aid of one young draftsman. It was a light, low-cost design based around a simple (though somewhat flexible) channel-section chassis, with a basic wood-framed fabric body on top. What little power there was came from a side-valve four-cylinder engine which displaced just 696cc when the car was announced in the fall of 1922. However, by the time the 'Seven Horse' went into production the following year, it had been given an enlarged engine of 747cc developing 10.5bhp. The tiny in-line four-cylinder engine was built to be as cheap as possible, its spindly crankshaft rotating in only two main bearings (one at each end) and lubricated by a crude 'spit and hope' oil system. Curiously, though the chassis and engine were simplistic, the Seven did sport front-wheel drum brakes at a time when many manufacturers still restricted braking to the rear wheels only – the big sporting Bentleys, for instance, didn't adopt four-wheel brakes until the following year.

The Seven provided what Austin liked to call 'Motoring for the Millions,' and at just £165 it cost little more than a motorcycle and sidecar combination but offered far better weather protection, more space, more comfort, and greater safety. Better still, the driver and passengers could travel in a real motor car rather than an augmented motorcycle, which pushed them a little higher up the social scale than their neighbors. To a British public which generally regarded motor cars as the preserve of the wealthy, the Seven opened up a whole new set of possibilities, just as Henry Ford's Model T had done in America a decade earlier. The middle classes took to the Seven in their thousands.

In addition to the streams of Sevens emerging from Austin's vast works at Longbridge, near Birmingham, the Seven would go on to be built in France (as the Rosengart), in Japan (as a Datsun), and in the United States (by American Austin). And it would enter production at Eisenach late in 1927 as the Dixi 3/15PS DA-1. 'DA' denoted Deutsche Ausführung or 'German version,' while the 3/15PS nomenclature indicated that the car had a three-speed

gearbox and developed 15 *pferdestarke*, the German equivalent of horsepower. With a price tag as low as 2750 Reichmarks, the new model cost less than half that of the bigger Dixis of the mid-'20s and only a little more than a BMW motorcycle (which cost around 2200 reichsmarks). In Britain the Austin Seven had attracted attention from makers of special bodies such as Swallow, and in Germany the Dixi, too, could be ordered with special bodies by coachbuilders such as Büschel. Many of the cars were supplied with fetching two-tone paint schemes with the fenders and running boards finished in a contrasting color to the body.

Above: *Closed sedan and open tourer bodystyles were both popular on the Dixi 3/15. There were even van versions.*

Just as BMW motorcycles had been spectacularly successful in competitive events, so the Dixi cars performed well in the races, hillclimbs, and reliability trials of the time. In the early days Dixis, like most other makes, were used very much in standard form, but as Dixi's racing activities were expanded after the World War I so the cars became more specialized, with modified engines and special racing bodywork. At the Grunewald Races in Berlin in 1921, 6/18PS Dixis took first and second places and they won second and third in their class at the first race at the Avus circuit in 1921. Four-cylinder 6/24 models then took over, sporting minimalist streamlined bodies. These cars won the team prize at the 1924 Reichsfahrt race and two 6/24s set an unofficial world record by completing a 20,000km (12,430-mile) run at Avus over the course of 16 days.

As sales began to drop in the 1920s the Dixis became less frequent competitors, but the tiny 3/15 soon brought the Eisenach company back to motor sport. The German Austin Seven derivative proved just as much at home on the track as the adaptable British Seven had done, though there were sadly no German equivalents of the jewel-like Austin Seven racing cars designed in Britain by Murray Jamieson for Austin's works team. Even so, major sporting successes for the Dixi came as early as 1928: in June that year the Dixi team for the 3000km (1864-mile) International Alpine Tour reached the finish without incurring any penalty points, a feat equaled by only one other team in the event. In September 1928 a team of four smart DA-1s took the first four places in their class at the ADAC Avus race, underlining the Dixi's speed and reliability compared to other small cars of the day.

Above: *The Austin Seven, and its derivative the Dixi 3/15, were powered by this simple two-bearing four-cylinder engine.*

Above: Dixi DA-2s in production at the Berlin-Johannisthal factory in 1929. The steel bodies were built by Ambi-Budd in Berlin.

Right: The first DA-2 leaving the factory in 1929. This model would become the first car to wear the BMW badge.

BMW buys Dixi

By 1928, then, the Dixi-Werke (as the Eisenach factory was now known) had weathered the economic storm and had begun to build cars which were popular and profitable. Further, the cars emerging from Eisenach were making a name for themselves in competition. But the picture wasn't all rosy: despite record production figures for a profitable new line of cars, the company was still sinking under the debts it had incurred before the 3/15 came along. BMW's board might have thought twice about investing in the Dixi-Werke once it understood the level of debts it would have to take on, but in the end the fact that industrialist Jakob Schapiro was a prominent presence on both companies' boards (he also had interests in several other German car makers) helped the deal to go through. By the end of 1928 the Dixi-Werke in Eisenach had become a subsidiary of BMW in Munich, and in March 1929 a new version of the Dixi 3/15, the DA-2, became the first car to wear the blue and white badge of BMW.

While the Dixi DA-1 had been almost identical to the Austin Seven on which it was based (in fact the first few *were* Sevens, brought over from England and sold as Dixis) the DA-2 had a host of improvements to the basic design, even if it was still recognizably Austin-based. Chief among the changes was a new all-steel body after the manner of the French Rosengart, with much bigger doors extending all the way down to the running boards and rearward over the top of the rear wheel arch, providing a much larger opening and consequently making ingress and egress considerably easier. Like many other all-steel bodies being introduced in Germany at the time, the DA-2 body was built at the vast Ambi-Budd factory which had been established in Berlin by Edward G. Budd, a leading proponent of steel bodies in America. It was probably to avoid transport costs that BMW leased a factory from Ambi-Budd at the nearby Berlin-Johannisthal airfield, where the first DA-2 models were assembled on March 29, 1929. But the new BMW wasn't immediately seen in public: the official launch of the car didn't take place until July that year, at the new BMW showroom in Berlin.

Left: The DA-2 was still based on the Austin Seven, but numerous improvements had been made to the design.

Above: The Dixi appeared in many rallies and trials in the 1920s and 1930s.

The 'Neue BMW Kleinwagen,' BMW's new small car, scored its first major competition victory in the International Alpine Trial of 1929, when three modified 3/15s brought the team prize home to Eisenach with an average speed of 26mph/h (42km). The following year a 3/15 took a class win in the Monte Carlo Rally, an event already famed as a test of men and machines.

Before long an open tourer version of the DA-2 was in production at Eisenach, retaining the old-fashioned style of body construction using a wood frame covered in doped fabric. BMW then expanded the range with the introduction of a DA-3 roadster, known as the 'Wartburg Sport,' recycling a name which had been used on some of Eisenach's earliest cars and on bicycles before that (and which was derived from Wartburg Castle, which overlooks the town of Eisenach). The Wartburg Sport was a popular model thanks to an uprated 18bhp engine which gave it a top speed of 53mph (85km/h) – considerably more than the 40mph (64km/h) or so of which the basic DA-1 had been capable. Attractive styling with a fold-flat windshield, cutaway sides and a narrow tail helped the Wartburg Sport to find around 400 buyers.

But despite some healthy sales, BMW struggled to pay off the debts it had inherited along with the acquisition of the Dixi-Werke, and business was not improved by the slump in the market that coincided with the great depression of 1929. Fortunately BMW's products were now more in tune with the times: the demand for motorcycles and the kind of frugal motor cars that BMW was building suffered far less than the market for more ostentatious motor cars such as those Dixi had once made. As a result BMW was in as good a position as anyone in the German motor industry to ride out the tough years of the early 1930s.

The last of the BMW models to be based around the Austin Seven design was the DA-4 of 1932, which saw further departures from the Austin design. Swing-axle independent front suspension appeared at the front, replacing the rigid forged-steel front axle which had been used on the earlier cars. The rigid axle had been prone to front wheel vibration, caused by the gyroscopic effects of the spinning wheels as the axle moved up and down over bumps in the road. In theory the independent front end of the DA-4 should have offered an

BMW Dixi DA-3 'Wartburg Sport'	
Production	1931-32
Engine	In-line four-cylinder, eight side valves, cast iron cylinder block and head
Bore x stroke	56mm x 76.2mm
Capacity	747cc
Power	18bhp at approximately 2400rpm
Torque	Not quoted
Fuel system	Single updraft carburetor
Gearbox	Three-speed manual, single dry-plate clutch
Chassis/body	Steel channel-section chassis with wood body frame and fabric covering
Suspension	Front: rigid front axle with radius arms and transverse leaf spring
	Rear: live axle with cantilever leaf springs
Brakes	Drums all round
Performance	Top speed: approximately 53mph (85km/h)

Above: The successful Dixi 3/15 team from the 1929 International Alpine Tour, an event in which the little cars excelled.

Below: By 1931, when this BMW Dixi was built, the design was nearing the end of its production life.

Right: The Wartburg roadster had an uprated engine, making it considerably quicker than the sedan versions.

improvement in ride and road behavior to offset its extra complication. In practice the swing-axles merely introduced camber changes to the front wheels as they went up and down over bumps, creating a different set of undesirable handling traits.

But in any case the DA-4 would only enjoy a short career as a front-line BMW model. The Bavarians ended their Austin connections in 1932, ceasing production of Seven-based cars after nearly 16,000 had been produced. Instead they turned their attention to a new car that had already been designed entirely in-house, with a radical new chassis, a refined version of the independent suspension system, and a new engine that was more sophisticated and more powerful than before. This car would herald a new era for the company, and the models that were to follow would lead BMW to still greater heights.

Boxer delights: BMW's first motorcycles

BMW ANNOUNCED its first motorcycle, the R32, at the Berlin Motor Show in 1923. Where previous BMW-powered machines like the Victoria had mounted the 'boxer' engine with the crankshaft across the frame and the cylinders fore and aft, the BMW design mounted the short but wide flat-twin engine with the crankshaft along the length of the machine with the cylinders sticking out on either side of the frame. This helped cool the cylinders, which stuck out into the air stream, and kept the machine's center of gravity low. The BMW's transmission was different from that of a conventional machine like the Victoria, too, with the

Above: A fine example of the R32, BMW's first serious motorcycle.

gearbox mounted on the back of the engine and drive to the rear wheel by shaft rather than the Victoria's chain. Another innovation was the use of telescopic front forks, a first for a motorcycle of this sort, and the R32's basic layout set the pattern for most of the two-wheeled BMWs produced right up to the present day.

A year later BMW introduced the R37, with a more powerful overhead valve engine developed by chief test engineer Rudolf Schleicher – a machine which won the German championship in 1924 in the hands of Franz Bieber. Further expansion of the BMW motorcycle range included the introduction in 1925 of the single-cylinder R39 (a 250cc sports machine with an output of 6.5bhp) and the 750cc R62 and R63 in 1927.

The R32 and its successors, built in an area separated by wooden fencing from the production line for aircraft engines which were once again being built in Munich, proved immensely successful. The first five years of production saw nearly 28,000 BMW motorcycles hit German roads, and the BMW machines won more than 500 races and

Above: BMW followed up the R32 motorcycle with this, the R37. With a more powerful overhead-valve engine, it proved to be a formidable racing machine, winning the German championship in 1924.

trials. Schleicher himself won a Gold Medal in the Six-Day Offroad Trials in Britain in 1926, the first for a German machine and rider, while in 1929 Ernest Henne used a 750cc BMW to set a new world speed record for motorcycles of 134mph (216km/h) on the Ingolstädter Langstrasse main road near Munich. The sales success of the motorcycles, coupled with strong demand for BMW engines, put the company on a firm financial footing for the first time since the cessation of hostilities in 1918.

Left: American Austin was another company to build the Austin Seven under license.

SPORTS CAR
SUCCESSES
1930-45

BMW 303

Production	1933-34
Engine	In-line six cylinder, 12 overhead valves, cast iron cylinder head
Bore x stroke	56mm x 80mm
Capacity	1182cc
Power	30bhp at 4000rpm
Torque	Not quoted
Fuel system	Twin Solex carburetors
Gearbox	Four-speed manual, single dry-plate clutch
Chassis/body	Tubular steel chassis with separate steel body
Suspension	Front: wishbone with transverse leaf spring Rear: live axle with leaf springs
Brakes	Drums all round
Performance	Top speed: approximately 55mph (89km/h)

Above: BMW departed from the Austin Seven design with the bigger 3/20 AM-1, of 1932.

Previous pages: Ernest Henne won the 1936 Eifelrennen sports car race in a BMW 328 – the car's first public appearance.

BMW CARS left their humble Austin-based roots firmly behind in 1932 with the introduction of new models which were wholly engineered in Munich. With this new line of cars BMW would build on the already impressive reputation of the Dixis and expand its range from one basic car (with several different body styles) to a much wider collection of cars with different engines, chassis, and overall sizes. The 1930s cars built at Eisenach would not only be best sellers and race winners, they would also help to influence car design well after the World War II.

The first of this new breed of all-German cars was the 3/20PS AM-1, AM standing for 'Ausführung München 1' or 'Munich Version 1.' Unlike the previous BMWs with their 747cc side-valve engines, AM-1 had a slightly larger 785cc in-line four – still related to the old Austin Seven design, but this time with overhead valves operated by pushrods and rockers. As the '20PS' designation indicated power output was up slightly compared to the old 3/15 (both cars being named after their horsepower 'class' rather than the actual output) and this pushed the sedan version's top speed up to 50mph (80km/h).

Previously BMW had used a chassis design similar to that of the Austin Seven with two simple channel-section members arranged in an A-shape, the apex being at the front of the car. For the AM-1, BMW introduced a completely new backbone chassis which owed nothing to the Austin design, using a single I-section beam which stretched from just behind the gearbox all the way to the tail of the car, with two outriggers arranged at the front to provide space for the engine and gearbox. The rear portion of the beam was kinked up and over the rear suspension and final drive unit. Though the swing-axle suspension of the DA-4 had proved problematic, the layout was retained at both ends of this new car but with the addition of transverse leaf springs to help iron out the less desirable effects of the geometry. In addition to its technical refinements, the 3/20 offered larger bodies (built by the Daimler-Benz body plant at Sindelfingen, near Stuttgart) with considerably better interior space and much greater comfort than the old cars. The sedan version was now a genuine family car: the Seven-derived sedans had all been fitted with four seats, but the 3/20 proved much less of a squeeze for a full complement of passengers.

The 3/20's greater size had been prompted by market demand, which was moving away from very small, very cheap cars. While the 3/20 continued in various improved forms until 1934, it became more and more obvious that BMW's customers were getting ever more prosperous and that more power would be needed for bigger and faster future models. To deliver greater power output Max Friz proposed building a completely new engine, a radical all-alloy in-line four. Rudolf Schleicher, who had left BMW for Horch in 1927 but had returned in 1933, suggested instead that two cylinders could be added to the existing in-line four to make a straight six: because it would have much in common with the existing four-cylinder engine, it could use some existing parts and tooling, making it relatively cheap and easy to make. Of the two proposals, Schleicher's six made more sense, but even so Friz took umbrage and left BMW soon after. When the six saw the light of day in 1934, it had been given twin carburetors and developed 30bhp from 1.2liters.

Rather than deploy this new engine in a development of the existing 3/20, BMW instead created a new car, the 303. This was based on another new chassis, this time a tubular A-frame with a 94.5in (2400mm) wheelbase. The change was prompted by more suspension work: at the front the leaf-spring now sat above a pair of wishbones to locate the wheels

and steadiness.' Despite the much bigger body and inevitably greater weight, the more powerful engine ensured that the 326 was still reasonably swift and it was certainly refined, so for the first time it meant that BMW had a car to challenge anything available from the might of Mercedes-Benz. Munich's first foray into the big luxury car market proved a successful one with more than 15,000 326 models built by the time production came to an end in 1939.

328: A masterpiece

By contrast the 328 of 1936 would be built in far smaller numbers, fewer than 500 leaving the production lines by 1939. Even so, the 328 became by far the best known and most respected of the pre-war BMWs, and one of the greatest sports cars of all in the inter-war years. Its styling was one reason: the flowing curves and business-like absence of decoration were a clear development of previous BMW sports cars, and the 328 managed to combine elegant proportions and a purposeful air to greater effect than any previous BMW. But it was aerodynamics, rather than aesthetics, that shaped the 328: those gentle curves and the lack of body adornments helped cut wind resistance, reducing the amount of power required to drive the car at high speed. Spats were available to cover the rear wheel openings to reduce drag further, something of a 1930s fashion. Aerodynamic considerations were also the reason why the headlamps were integrated into the bodywork at the front of the car for the first time, giving the 328 a distinctive, modern face as well as a more streamlined shape. Behind the now-familiar twin-kidney grille – which in this case curved gently backward toward the top – a pair of leather straps retained a long, louvered hood under which sat a new development of the six-cylinder engine. Development engineer Rudolf Schleicher sought to improve the engine's efficiency, but without resorting to the complicated and costly twin-overhead-camshaft layouts that were becoming fashionable in racing engines.

Twin-overhead-camshaft engines generally develop more power than equivalent overhead-valve engines because the layout offers a number of advantages. The classic arrangement is to use a combustion chamber which is hemispherical (or more often slightly less than half a sphere, which should properly be termed 'part-spherical') and which contains two (or more) opposed valves.

One camshaft of the pair operates the row of inlet valves on one side of the engine, and the other camshaft operates the row of exhaust valves on the other side. Given a single spark plug at the top, the hemispherical combustion chamber gives the engine good thermal efficiency because its shape encourages the air and fuel mixture to burn fully. Allied to well-shaped intake and exhaust ports, the opposed valve layout gives the engine a free-breathing nature, improving what engine designers term 'volumetric' efficiency. The low inertia of the valve gear in a twin-overhead-cam

BMW 326	
Production	1936-41
Engine	In-line six cylinder, 12 overhead valves, cast iron cylinder head
Bore x stroke	66mm x 96mm
Capacity	1971cc
Power	50bhp at 3750rpm
Torque	Not quoted
Fuel system	Twin Solex carburetors
Gearbox	Four-speed manual, single dry-plate clutch
Chassis/body	Box-section steel chassis with separate steel body
Suspension	Front: Wishbone and transverse leaf spring Rear: Live axle and torsion bars
Brakes	Drums all round
Performance	Top speed: approximately 72mph (116km/h)

Below: Special Beutler bodywork makes this 328 look more modern than it is – it was built in 1937.

BMW 328

Production	1936–39
Engine	In-line six cylinder, 12 overhead valves, aluminum alloy cylinder head with opposed valves operated by pushrods.
Bore x stroke	66mm x 96mm
Capacity	1971cc
Power	80bhp at 5000rpm
Torque	96lbft at 4000rpm
Fuel system	Triple downdraft Solex carburetors
Gearbox	Four-speed manual, single dry-plate clutch
Chassis/body	Tubular steel chassis, steel body with aluminum alloy hood, trunk-lid and doors
Suspension	Front: wishbone and transverse leaf spring Rear: live axle with leaf springs
Brakes	Drums all round
Performance	Top speed: approximately 95mph (153km/h) 0-60mph (0-97km/h): approximately 10.5sec

engine, meanwhile, allows it to run to higher rotational speeds. All these factors combine to ensure that the engine can make the most of its capacity and provide a high power output.

What Schleicher did was to adopt a new light-alloy cylinder head for the existing straight-six BMW engine, with an efficient part-spherical combustion chamber and opposed valves, just like in a twin-cam head. Schleicher then arranged a novel system for operating all the valves from the original camshaft, still mounted low down on one side of the engine block. The inlet valves were larger than before, at 35mm diameter instead of 30mm, and were operated by pushrods and rockers just as they were in the earlier engine. The valve gear for each 32mm exhaust valve also began with a vertical pushrod and a rocker on the intake side of the engine, but from there a short horizontal 'cross pushrod' transferred the motion across the top of the engine, and finally another rocker on the far side of the head operated the valve itself. The engine thus had a rocker cover on each side of the cylinder head, which made it look, as well as perform, a bit like a twin-cam unit. Schleicher's system could not compete with the high-revving ability of a good twin-cam set-up thanks to all the valve-gear ironmongery going up and down and back and forth, but the long-stroke straight-six was never likely to be a high-revving engine anyway, so the potential drawback was more theoretical than practical.

More power, less weight

While the usual layout of a twin-cam head has horizontal ports, the 328 engine had vertical intake ports and horizontal exhausts. Three downdraft Solex carburetors sat on top, each one delivering mixture to the siamesed intake ports of a pair of cylinders. The result was a 2.0-liter engine producing 80bhp, considerably more than even super-tuned versions of the previous 1.9-liter engine had managed. In racing trim the new engine could now be persuaded to deliver up to 135bhp, and had war not intervened, BMW would have fielded a version with fuel injection a good dozen years before Mercedes-Benz would go the same route with its 300SL. But despite the impressive power of this normally-aspirated 2.0-liter engine, the 328 was also subjected to an extensive program of weight-saving to ensure competitive performance against some of the powerful supercharged opposition. A lightweight version of the 303's tubular frame was developed, and light alloy body panels were fitted to keep the overall weight to around 1764lb (800kg).

The first public appearance of the new car was at the Nürburgring for the Eifelrennen sports car race on June 14, 1936. The racers were in the hands of Ernst Henne, holder of the motorcycle world speed record (on a BMW, of course) and Uli Richter. Henne won the class with Richter third, beginning an unrivaled career for the 328 in sports car racing in the years leading up to World War II. Serious production began in 1937, and from then until the outbreak of war in 1939 the 328 was regularly seen in German sports car events where it often trounced much more powerful opposition. The 328's advantages were its excellent power-to-weight ratio and the predictable handling afforded by its relatively soft suspension, in an era when most sports cars were crashy, hard-riding affairs which struggled to keep all their wheels on the ground at the same time. *The Autocar* was astonished by the comfortable ride delivered by the 328's independent front suspension, at the same time praising the BMW's 'outstanding cornering' but expressing some concern at what the reviewer saw as over-light steering.

Such was the 328's popularity as a sports-racing car that some events saw the grids dominated by BMWs – for example at the German Grand Prix meeting in 1938, when the first four rows of the grid were entirely populated by 328s. It was hardly worth anything else turning up. Outside Germany, too, the 328 proved very successful, with class wins in most of the major sports car races. A trio of green 328s driven by H.J. Aldington, 'B. Bira' (a pseudonym of Siamese Prince Birabongse Bhanutej Bhanubandh) and A.F.P. Fane brought

Below: This 1938 BMW 321 is effectively a short-wheelbase 326. BMW's numbering system became more and more confusing in the 1930s.

Above: H.J. Aldington sold BMWs in Britain as Frazer Nash-BMWs. This is a 328.

Opposite: The 1938 BMW 328 raced by Betty Haig, one of the most famous women racing drivers of the 1930s.

Below: The cross-pushrod engine had many of the advantages of a twin-cam unit.

Right: The clean lines of the 328 were aerodynamically efficient, as well as attractive.

home the team prize in the 1936 Ulster Tourist Trophy, the last to be run on the magnificent Ards road course, with Fane a fine third to the Freddie Dixon/Charles Dodson Riley and Eddie Hall's Bentley. The following weekend Fane appeared in his TT car at Shelsley Walsh, the famous hillclimb, and proceeded to post the fastest sports-car time of the day. In April 1937 S.C.H. Davis, redoubtable racer and Sports Editor of *The Autocar*, put 102.22 miles (164.51km) into an hour at the Brooklands race track in a race-prepared 328 with a best lap at 103.97mph (167.32km/h). Later that year 'Bira' took the 328 to a class win and another third place overall in the Tourist Trophy, which had moved to the Donington circuit following accidents at Ards in previous years. Numerous successes followed in British sports car racing at Brooklands and at other venues, with Fane and Aldington always to the fore.

France was a less successful hunting ground for BMW, to start with at least. In the 1936 French Grand Prix at Montlhéry, for sports cars that year, a team of three 328s led the 2.0-liter class comfortably until mechanical problems intervened and all three were forced to retire. The 328 did not appear in the Le Mans 24-hour race until 1937 (the 1936 race had been canceled due to strikes in France), and it proved no more successful there than it had been at Montlhéry. During the course of the 24 hours, Aldington and Fane retired with engine trouble, while the cars of David Murray/Pat Fairfield and Fritz Roth/Uli Richter were both eliminated in accidents – one of which claimed the life of Fairfield after a multiple shunt at the White House corner. In Italy the 328s fared better, with two cars appearing in the top 10 of the Mille Miglia in 1937, Fane/James eighth and Lurani/Schaumburg-Lippe 10th, less than a minute behind the ninth-placed Alfa Romeo of Cortese and Fumagalli after nearly 14 hours of racing. But like Le Mans in 1937 and the TT in 1936, the 1937 Mille Miglia was a tragic race: the Lancia Aprilia of Bruzzo and Mignanego somersaulted into the crowd after crossing a tramline just after leaving Bologna, killing ten people. As a result the epic 1000-mile dash around Italy was banned from using public roads and could not be held in 1939. Instead there was a Tobruk-Tripoli race across North Africa, 328s filling the first three places in the 2.0-liter sports car class.

Frazer Nash: the English BMWs

Captain Archibald Frazer Nash founded the company bearing his name in 1924, building tough little sports cars with 1.5-liter Anzani engines and chain-drive to the rear axle. The company was taken over by promoter, driver, engineer, and entrepreneur H.J. Aldington in 1929, and he continued with the increasingly old-fashioned Frazer Nash, fitting ever larger and more powerful engines.

Aldington also ran the cars in competition, and it was at the Alpine Trial in 1934 that he came up against a well-organized team of BMW 315s, which beat the Frazer Nash cars to the team prize in the event. Impressed, Aldington did a deal with BMW's Franz Josef Popp to sell right-hand-drive BMW cars in Britain, starting with the 315 and later progressing to the 328, which made as big an impression in the UK as it had done in Germany. Most of the cars arrived at the Frazer Nash works (in Isleworth, West London) fully built, though some were bodied in Britain. Badges were changed and the steering swapped from left- to right-hand-drive, but otherwise the cars were very much the way BMW intended.

After the war it was Aldington who arranged for BMW car and engine designs to be sold to Bristol as war reparations, the result being BMW-derived Bristol cars which began production in 1947 and the supply of BMW-based Bristol engines to Frazer Nash, AC, Lotus, and others. Aldington continued with a new line of Frazer Nash cars based on a development of the BMW 328 chassis and these continued until the late 1950s, and thereafter AFN, the owner of the brand, concentrated on selling cars rather than making them. The Frazer Nash-BMW was revived in the 1960s as a luxury version of the Neue Klasse sedan, but then the Frazer Nash marque was gone for good.

Above: Bristol's version of the BMW straight-six was substantially reworked.

Top: *The Frazer Nash Targa Florio was based on the pre-war BMW 328.*

Left: *Full-width bodywork was essential under new Le Mans regulations.*

Streamlined roadster bodies appeared on the 328s at Le Mans in 1938, winning the class in the 24-hour race, and in the RAC Tourist Trophy at Donington later that year, the Frazer Nash 328s of Aldington and Fane were joined by a third car for Dick Seaman. The tall, dashing Seaman was making his name as a Mercedes-Benz Grand Prix driver at the time, and had just proposed to Franz Josef Popp's daughter Erica. The pair would marry in London that December – but the unlucky Seaman would die at Spa in Belgium in a Grand Prix Mercedes just six months later.

Above: Streamlined 328s, in open and closed form, ran in competition in the years leading up to World War II.

Final victory

The streamlined roadsters were joined by a closed 'sedan' version for the 1940 Mille Miglia, which was a shortened race run on a closed circuit around Brescia under the title of the 'Gran Premio Brescia della Mille Miglia.' Race organizer Conte Aymo Maggi visited BMW directors at the Berlin Motor Show to persuade them to field a works team, so ensuring the race's 'international' status. BMW did send a team, and the race was won by Baron Huschke von Hanstein and Walter Baumer in a very special lightweight 328 coupé at an average of more than 100mph with more works BMWs third, fifth, and sixth. The bodies were built by Touring of Milan on their Superleggera principles, an ultra-lightweight body construction technique using a network of small-diameter tubes welded together to form a body frame which supported panels made of 'Elektron' alloy. The body weighed just 95lb (43kg) and the whole car tipped the scales around 1430lb (650kg), some 330lb (150kg) lighter than the standard 328. The light, low-drag body enabled the Mille Miglia 328 to reach a top speed of 134mph (216km/h), and brought home for the first time the aerodynamic advantages of a fixed-roof car rather than an open roadster – the BMW 'sedan' was 6mph (10km/h) quicker

Above: The 327 was available with the highly-tuned 328 engine, as in this 1939 car.

Above: The flowing lines of the 327 coupé would inspire post-war Bristols.

Above right: Another 328-engined 327. The two-tone paintwork was popular in the 1930s.

Right: The 335 of 1939 was the biggest BMW yet, paving the way for the palatial sedans the company would build in post-war years.

BMW 335

Production	1939-41
Engine	In-line six cylinder, 12 overhead valves, aluminum alloy cylinder head.
Bore x stroke	82mm x 110mm
Capacity	3485cc
Power	90bhp at 3500rpm
Torque	Not quoted
Fuel system	Solex carburetor
Gearbox	Four-speed manual, single dry-plate clutch
Chassis/body	Box-section steel chassis with separate steel body
Suspension	Front: wishbone and transverse leaf spring Rear: live axle and torsion bars
Brakes	Drums all round
Performance	Top speed: approximately 90mph (145km/h)

than the open version. Mercedes-Benz applied the same principles when it came to design its Le Mans-winning 300SL racing car in the early 1950s, opting for a low-drag fixed-roof car when most of the competition still persisted with roadsters. Incidentally, the Mille Miglia-winning coupé made its way to America in the mid-1950s. Thirty years later it was bought and restored by California car collector Jim Proffitt, and is now seen promoting BMW at historic car events all over the world.

While the 328 won plaudits on the race track, it was the big BMWs which were winning orders in the showrooms. The 326 was joined by a mystifying line-up of models which mixed and matched BMW's engines, bodies, and chassis. For a short time there was a 329 using the 326 drophead body but the older tubular frame and a lower-power engine, followed by a 320 which used a shorter version of the 326 body and the simpler suspension of the 319. Despite the indications *The Motor* still praised the car it tested for its 'very good combination of comfortable riding and accurate road holding.' In 1938 the 320 was superseded by the 321, which retained the shorter body but now used the better suspension system of the 326.

Similar in concept was the 327, a coupé or convertible version of the 326 sharing the 321's shorter wheelbase and fitted with the 55bhp 1.9-liter engine. It was also briefly available with the 80bhp 328 engine, in which form it was known, confusingly, as the 327/28. As war loomed BMW introduced one final sedan model, the 335, which was even bigger than the 326 with a 117.3in (2980mm) wheelbase. Power came from a 3.5-liter straight-six engine developing 90bhp, making BMW's new sedan just about the last word in comfort and space. But priorities changed once war was declared in September 1939, and after just a few hundred 335s had been built, the BMW factories were turned over to war work.

War work

During the war BMW continued to make vehicles and engines, but now under contract to the German government. The R75 motorcycle combination used a 26PS 748cc flat-twin engine and with a driven wheel on the sidecar as well as on the motorcycle, it proved to be incredibly agile on rough ground. Around 16,000 were built for the German forces, who also received the BMW 325, a heavy-duty four-wheel-drive truck. In Munich production of aero-engines was stepped up, BMW supplying V12s for the Messerschmitt Bf 109 fighter aircraft and radial engines for the triple-engined Junkers Ju 52 transport/bomber. BMW also took over Bramo, a Brandenburg engine factory, which was developing a gas turbine engine for use in the Messerschmitt Me 262 jet fighter, and the company was involved in the development of rocket motors for missiles.

The end of the war brought virtual ruin for BMW, though the company would recover, just, and BMW cars would again be built – this time in Munich rather than Eisenach. But despite the troubles that the company would have to weather, BMW continued to enjoy a considerable reputation in motor racing thanks to the enduring 328. The 328 not only won one of the last races before the war put paid to motor racing, it also won one of the first to be

Below: This 328 coupé won the shortened 1940 Mille Miglia. It was restored in America in the 1980s.

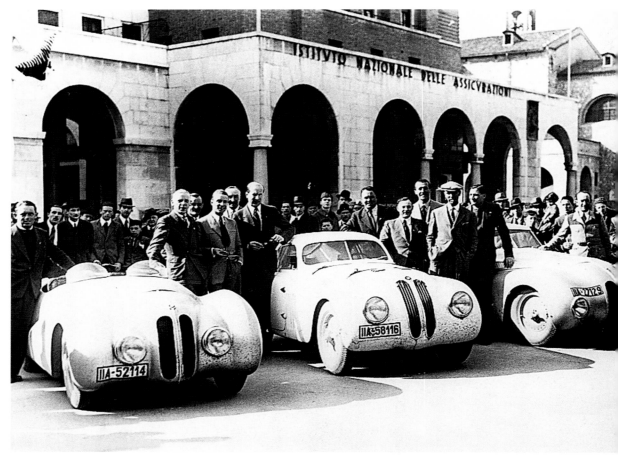

Above: One of the Touring-bodied 328s crosses another finishing line.

Top: At Le Mans the coupés were quicker down the Mulsanne straight than the open 328s, thanks to their superior aerodynamics.

Right: The 1940 Mille Miglia BMWs, with the winning coupé in the center.

Flying high: BMW's aero-engines

The Type IIIa BMW engine had been Munich's first successful aero-engine, and many more followed. The Type IV and Type V were water-cooled in-line sixes like the Type III, and they were followed by a series of V12s in ever-bigger capacities. In 1934 a new company, BMW Flugmotorenbau, was set up to manage the aero-engine side of the business and its first product was the 132, a nine-cylinder radial engine based on an American Pratt & Whitney design used under license. This went into the famous multi-role Junkers Ju 52, known variously as 'Iron Annie' or the 'Corrugated Coffin' thanks to its corrugated steel body: Junkers always went in for function rather than form.

The Type 139, a bigger version of the Pratt & Whitney design, proved unsuccessful, so instead BMW produced the 801, a vast 41.8-liter engine with two rows of seven cylinders, each with a bore and stroke of 156mm. The two rows of cylinders were mounted close together, and air-cooled by a magnesium fan which was geared to run at 1.72 times engine speed. A major advance was a device called the 'Kommandogerät,' an electro-hydraulic unit which automatically controlled fuel flow, mixture strength, ignition timing, and propeller pitch in response to the position of the pilot's throttle lever. On later engines with a two-stage supercharger the device also engaged the second stage of the supercharger if the aircraft was at sufficient altitude to need it. The 801 was fitted to the Focke-Wulf Fw 190, one of the most effective German fighters of World War II.

In 1939 BMW acquired the Brandenberg Motor Works, known as 'Bramo,' which

Above: The famous 'corrugated' Junkers Ju 52 was powered by BMW Type 132 radial engines.

was developing jet engines for the *Reichsluftfahrtministerium,* the German air ministry. Problems delayed the engine, and a Junkers unit was used in the Messerschmitt for which the '003 had been planned. Instead BMW's turbojet went into the Heinkel He 162, and it formed the basis for post-war jet development in France and the Soviet Union.

run after the cessation of hostilities in 1945. RAF Flight Lieutenant Tony Crook, who would become a partner in the Bristol car company in the mid-1960s, was a regular 328 racer and it was Crook's 328 which won the first motor race held in Britain since the war. In 1946 Leslie Johnson achieved a fine second place in the Belgian Grand Prix for sports cars, chasing home 'Jock' Horsfall's rapid pre-war Aston Martin and recording the fastest lap.

Memories of the streamlined 328 racers were still strong, and H.J. Aldington managed to bring one of them to Britain after the war by claiming it was his own 328 which had been crashed in Germany in the late 1930s and had to be left there during the war. After fitting the streamlined 328 with a new grille, he proclaimed it the 'new Frazer Nash,' and indeed post-war Frazer Nash cars would be based on the 328's chassis and streamlined bodywork. BMW itself had been thinking along similar lines, and it was only the war which put paid to a super-streamlined version of the 328 being released as a production car.

Above: A rare color photograph showing the BMW team arriving at Brescia during the 1940 Mille Miglia.

Those streamlined cars would also be the inspiration behind the styling of the Jaguar XK120 – one of the most influential sports cars of the 1940s, which made its debut at the first post-war London Motor Show in 1948. Echoes of those curvaceous lines would be seen all through the 1950s, on cars as diverse as the Triumph TR2 and the Chevrolet Corvette. During the war Jaguar had also been experimenting with a four-cylinder engine code-named XG with BMW-style cross-pushrod valve gear, though in the end it opted to fit twin overhead camshafts to its new range of XK six-cylinder engines.

It would take British sports car manufacturers years to get ahead of the 328s on the track, but even longer for BMW itself to return to the glories of the pre-war years. For BMW, the second half of the 1940s would be a difficult time, and the 1950s would be disastrous.

BAROQUE
ANGELS AND
BANKRUPTCY
1945-59

Previous pages: BMW launched its new
501 model at the Frankfurt Motor Show
in April 1951.

SURVIVAL WAS the best that BMW could hope for in the years immediately following World War II. Wartime bombing had reduced Munich to little more than rubble, and what remained had been taken over by the Allies, the American army using BMW's factories for vehicle maintenance. Mindful of BMW's role in supplying aircraft engines for the *Luftwaffe* and in developing jet and rocket motors, the Allies prohibited the Munich firm from re-entering the aircraft industry, and neither was it allowed to make cars. Even the manufacture of motorcycles was prohibited, and for the second time in living memory the Bavarian Motor Works was reduced to making everything but motors: Munich turned out cooking pots and farm machinery in an effort to keep the production lines busy, and later produced an aluminum-framed bicycle.

Tooling and parts for motorcycle production had been moved out of Munich to Eisenach in 1942, and the Eisenach factory had escaped major bomb damage. But now control of Germany was split between the occupying Allied forces, and the town of Eisenach found itself just inside the Soviet-controlled sector. The Soviets nationalized the Eisenach factory, and in 1945 they used BMW tooling to build motorcycles which were essentially BMW R35s. Cars soon followed, Eisenach building the pre-war BMW 321 and a slightly modified 327 mainly for export. A new 340 model also appeared, based on the big pre-war 326 sedan but fitted with a new and rather ungainly American-style radiator grille. All these cars were sold under the BMW badge, until buyers started demanding supplies of spare parts from Munich. BMW complained, and thereafter the East German cars adopted the name EMW (for 'Eisenacher Motoren Werke') and were fitted with a red and white version of the BMW roundel. Production of BMW-based cars in Eisenach ended in 1955 when the company changed its name to

Above: BMW motorcycle production restarted
in 1948 with the single-cylinder R24.

Automobilwerk Eisenach, its new product being the IFA F9 which had previously been built by another nationalized East German car maker, DKW, at Zwickau (later home of the Trabant). In 1956 the F9 was rebodied and renamed the Wartburg, reintroducing a name which had originally been used by Eisenach in the late 1890s and which BMW itself had used on a roadster in the late 1920s. The same mechanicals soldiered on until 1988 when a four-stroke engine was finally substituted. In the 1990s the factory came under Opel control after the unification of Germany.

Motorcycle production began at Munich in December 1948. BMW's activities were strictly controlled, and at first Munich was only allowed to build a small, single-cylinder motorcycle, the R24. Car production was always the goal, but this did not get under way until three years later and by then BMW engineering had appeared on the road in two other guises.

Above: BMW designs were adapted in Britain to produce the first Bristol road car, the 400 of 1949.

Left: The Dutch Cotura was based on BMW 328 mechanical parts, but with a lighter steel and aluminum alloy body.

H.J. Aldington, who had sold BMWs in Britain under the Frazer Nash-BMW banner, saw to it that the Bristol Aeroplane Company acquired BMW's pre-war designs as war reparations and also encouraged BMW engineer Fritz Fiedler to come to England to continue the cars' development. The result was the Bristol 400 of 1947. Meanwhile in Germany BMW engineers created specialist cars using 328 mechanicals. Ernst Loof and Lorenz Dietrich set themselves up under the name Veritas (Latin for 'truth') in the small town of Messkirch, 130 miles (210km) west of Munich, where they built road and racing cars based on the pre-war BMW 328 and using mostly second-hand parts. Karl Kling won the German 2.0-liter sports car championship in 1947, 1948, and 1949 with Veritas cars. Those parts were difficult to find, however, so Veritas went over to engines of its own design built by Heinkel. Despite the success of these cars the company over-reached itself and found itself in financial trouble by

Above: Veritas was started by two BMW engineers, building 328-based racing cars.

1950. Loof moved the company to the Nürburgring and concentrated on the racing side with more success, but in 1953 he returned to BMW and Veritas was no more.

Helmut Polensky was another BMW engineer to build a 328-based car, the Formula 2 Monopol. Despite the advanced design of the car, with a light tubular chassis frame and rear-mounted 328 engine, the project came to nothing. More successful was another Formula 2 car, the AFM, built by former BMW engineer Alex von Falkenhausen – 'AFM' was the combination of Falkenhausen's initials plus an 'M' for Munich. AFM's cars were also 328-based, and it was their spirited performances which would bring Falkenhausen to the attention of BMW. Before long he would rejoin BMW, setting up an in-house racing operation in 1954.

Above: Paul Greifzu's 328-based F2 car won a famous victory at Avus in 1951.

Munich rebuilds

Below: The first delivery of BMW 501s, took place in Munich in 1952.

Other German car makers were now back in business. Mercedes-Benz, up the road in Stuttgart, had recovered from the near total destruction of its factories to begin building its first post-war cars in 1947. Opel at Rüsselsheim, near Frankfurt, restarted production of the Olympia the same year, and announced the new Kapitän in 1948. Ferdinand Porsche had begun producing his own cars in a small way at Gmünd, Austria, in 1948 and by 1950 a proper production line had been set up in the Stuttgart suburb of Zuffenhausen. The occupying forces in Germany had been supplied with Volkswagens since the end of the war, and in 1949 production began for the general public in Wolfsburg. BMW, meanwhile, was

Bavarian Influences

BRISTOL TOOK the best bits of BMW's pre-war output – the accomplished 326 chassis, the powerful 328 cross-pushrod engine, and the stylish 327 two-door body – and combined them in an effective, if expensive, high-performance sedan, the 400 of 1947. Bristol's typically thorough approach to reworking the BMW designs included a complete review of the materials used in the suspension and engine. The company was putting to good use the expertise it had developed through years of aircraft and aero-engine design. The 400 was succeeded by the aerodynamically-shaped 401 (and drophead 402) in 1949. The 403 of 1953 was similar, but featured a host of detail revisions. Later the short-wheelbase 404 and four-door

405 still used the BMW-derived cross-pushrod six and the torsion-bar 326 suspension. The engine was expanded to 2216cc for the 406, but the 407 turned to a new power source (Chrysler's 5.2-liter V8) and new double-wishbone front suspension. Chrysler-powered Bristols continue in production today.

Bristol briefly turned to racing with the pushrod-engined 450, and supplied rolling chassis to S.H. 'Wacky' Arnolt in the US, who produced the Arnolt-Bristol which proved adept on the track. Bristol engines also went to AC for the Ace and Aceca, and to AFN for use in Frazer Nash cars. Aldington also used BMW's V8 engines in his Competition Model and Continental coupé, and some Frazer

Nashes sported the torsion-bar 326 suspension. But only small numbers of cars were ever made at Isleworth, production ending in 1957 – the same year that a small number of BMW V8-engined Lago Talbots were built at Suresnes in France.

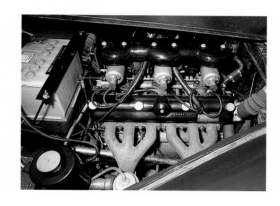

Above: The Bristol 400 engine was derived from the pre-war cross-pushrod 328 unit.

Left: The 400 combined the best elements of BMW's pre-war products into an impressive sporting sedan.

Above: It may be considered cramped by modern standards, but the 400 interior was beautifully made.

creating a new car production facility from almost nothing and with limited resources, and its post-war car production would not begin at Munich until 1951. There had been some debate within the company about the kind of car BMW should use to re-establish itself, and Fritz Fiedler (now returned to Munich from Bristol) proposed a tiny economy car powered by the BMW flat-twin motorcycle engine. But the board decided that BMW should capitalize on its reputation for building some of the finest pre-war German cars by again making big, powerful machines. It was these that would be launched at the first Frankfurt Motor Show in April 1951.

Above: With the 501 BMW continued its move upmarket, chasing the mighty Mercedes-Benz.

BMW 501

Production	1952-54
	(other derivatives 1954-58)
Engine	In-line six cylinder, 12 overhead valves, cast iron cylinder head.
Bore x stroke	66mm x 96mm
Capacity	1971cc
Power	65hp at 4000rpm
Torque	95lbft at 2000rpm
Fuel system	Twin-choke Solex 30PAAJ carburetor
Gearbox	Four-speed manual, single dry-plate clutch
Chassis/body	Steel chassis with box-section and tubular members, separate steel body
Suspension	Front: double wishbone and torsion bars Rear: live axle and torsion bars
Brakes	Hydraulically-operated drums all round
Performance	Top speed: 86mph (138km/h) 0-62mph (0-100km/h): 27sec

Opposite: While the 501, and the cars derived from it, were undoubtedly impressive, they did little to improve BMW's financial situation.

BMW's plush stand at the show was devoted to just a single car, a curvaceous black sedan that was longer and wider than the pre-war 326 – in fact 8in (200mm) bigger in both its length and its width. The imposing modern shape incorporated a squatter version of the BMW 'kidney' grille and a long hood leading to a large cabin with big doors and an extensive glass area. Under the skin of this part-complete prototype the engineering was largely that of the 326, which meant there was a hefty but strong chassis with large box-section side members. Torsion bar suspension was now used at both ends of the car and delivered a comfortable ride, and a stiffer sports suspension with 22mm diameter bars instead of 20.7mm was an option. Curious details included a 'pinion and sector' steering system, effectively a rack and pinion system with a curved rack, which was employed to allow space for the engine to be mounted far forward, in turn allowing all the seats to be positioned within the wheelbase for a supple ride. The engine, a 1971cc version of the pre-war straight-six, drove through a primary shaft to a remote gearbox (made by ZF at Friedrichshafen) which was mounted between the front seats, and that gave the typically German column gearchange a tortuous linkage and an ill-defined action. Right-hand-drive cars for Britain, still sold through AFN in Isleworth, had floor-mounted gear levers. Either way, the benefit of the remote gearbox was that the front floor of the cabin was flat and the front bench seat could accommodate three.

Though this new BMW, called the 501, was powered by much the same engine as the pre-war 326, further engine development meant that the 501 had 65bhp compared to the pre-war car's 50bhp, though even this struggled against the new car's all-up weight of some 2828lb (1285kg). Many sedans of the time, some of them with much smaller engines, were considerably livelier than the 501, though BMW had exciting engine developments on the horizon which would deal with that problem in due course.

Despite its lack of performance in comparison to other grand sedans of the era, the 501 won acclaim for the solidity of its engineering and the sheer extravagance of its design. At a little over 15,000 deutschmarks, the 501 cost four times as much as the average German earned in a year. It was almost 4000 deutschmarks more than its closest rival, the Mercedes-Benz 220 that had also been launched at Frankfurt in 1951. The Mercedes was quicker, if a little smaller and a lot less curvaceous, but the Stuttgart machine's biggest advantage was that it was readily available to buy, while all BMW could do was to take your order. Meanwhile development of the 501 dragged on, and production machines wouldn't become available until the end of 1952. Even then, the investment BMW had made (with money from the Deutsche Bank) in modern press-shop equipment had yet to bear fruit and the first 501 bodies were instead built by Baur near Stuttgart and sent to Munich to be mated with the chassis. The characteristic flowing curves of the 501's body soon earned it the nickname Barokengel or 'Baroque Angel,' because it reminded some people of the carved wooden figures found in the Baroque churches in Germany and Austria.

Once BMW finally managed to get the 501 into production, it found its troubles had just begun. Sales predicted for the big sedan had been wildly optimistic – the board expected to sell 3000 a year, but production averaged only 2000 or so during the vehicle's six years as a front-line model. Most Germans were getting about on bicycles, and some were buying motorized bicycles or motorcycles (healthy sales of which were helping to keep BMW going). The cars on the German roads at the time were mostly patched-up pre-war jobs, there being

few Germans with enough money to buy any sort of new car, let alone an expensive one like the 501. Worse still, those who could afford a posh new car could choose from two Mercedes models which neatly bracketed the 501: on the one hand there was the cheaper, swifter Mercedes-Benz 220 and on the other there was the bigger, plusher 300 so beloved of German chancellor Konrad Adenauer.

The 501 was given a much-needed shot in the arm in 1954. A bigger carburetor and a higher rev limit boosted the six-cylinder engine to 72hp, and this '501A' model went on sale at 14,180 deutschmarks – 1000 marks less than its predecessor. A further 1000-mark price cut came six months later. In addition, a simplified '501B' went on sale with the same engine and similar bodywork but lower levels of equipment – and a price tag another 1000 marks lower. But the big news for 1954 came at the other end of the range with a much more powerful new sister model.

Above: The 501 V8 (and the similar 502) offered pace and space, but – crucially for sales – they were expensive.

V8 Power

Since 1949 BMW had been working on a new V8 engine for its big sedans, and the result was a 2580cc engine with a central camshaft and overhead valves, developing 100bhp, which made its public debut at the Geneva Salon in March 1954. Clearly BMW's engine designers had taken notice of the new generation of V8s being introduced in America, pioneered by Cadillac and Oldsmobile. Germany's first post-war V8, the BMW engine was novel because of its extensive use of aluminum alloy. The crankcase and the cylinder heads were alloy, as were the cast sump, timing cover, intake manifold, and clutch housing. There were steel cylinder liners exposed to the coolant. Normally when 'wet' liners like this were used in an engine the waterways between adjacent cylinders would be open, and the whole crankcase would effectively be an open box. Often the block would lack

Above: In 1955 the 501 was offered with a V8 engine, making it one of Germany's fastest sedan cars.

stiffness, and the result would be short engine life. BMW avoided the problem by giving each liner its own individual waterways with webs cast into the aluminum between the liners: the result was greater stiffness, making the engine smooth and reliable and once again demonstrating the engine design abilities of the Bayerische Motoren Werke.

The V8-engined 502 looked much the same as the six-cylinder 501, except along the waistline, while it had a more luxurious interior. Performance, however, was in a different league: while the six-cylinder 501 was one of the most sedate German sedans, the V8 502 was one of the quickest, with a 50mph (0-80km/h) acceleration time of around 11 seconds, a clear five seconds quicker than the 501. In 1955 the 502 was given wrap-around rear windows and a long-stroke 3.2-liter V8 engine, producing 120bhp. The short-stroke 2.6-liter V8 then went into the 501 to produce the 501 V8, which ran alongside the six-cylinder car (now bored out to 2077cc). But demand for the sixes tailed off dramatically: buyers with that

BMW 502

Production	1954-58
	(other derivatives 1958-64)
Engine	All-alloy 90-degree V8, 16 overhead valves
Bore x stroke	74mm x 75mm
Capacity	2580cc
Power	100hp at 4800rpm
Torque	133lbft at 2500rpm
Fuel system	Twin-choke Solex 30PAAJ carburetor
Gearbox	Four-speed manual, single dry-plate clutch
Chassis/body	Steel chassis with box-section and tubular members, separate steel body
Suspension	Front: double wishbone and torsion bars
	Rear: live axle and torsion bars
Brakes	Hydraulically-operated drums all round
Performance	Top speed: 100mph (160km/h) 0-62mph (0-100km/h):15.5sec

sort of money wanted more performance and were prepared to pay more for the V8, while the less wealthy satisfied themselves with the much cheaper, but equally fast, Opel Kapitän. Series production of the six-cylinder 501 finally ended in 1958, the last few adopting the 'panorama' rear window of the 502. Munich continued to assemble the odd six-cylinder car for the Bavarian police and fire services over the next few years.

Special-bodied versions of both the 501 and 502 kept German coachbuilders busy during the 1950s and into the '60s, some turning the big BMW sedans into ambulances and hearses (while the Mindener Karrosseriefabrik built buses with BMW V8 engines). Coupés and cabriolets were also built, these rare and richly-appointed machines being produced in tiny numbers for the privileged rich. Even so, BMW felt that there was a market for faster, better-looking and inevitably more expensive derivatives of the V8s – and that market was the USA.

BMWs were now being imported into America by Max Hoffman, an Austrian émigré who had set up in business in the 1940s importing European sports cars. Hoffman had sold thousands of MGs, and had brought Jaguar and Porsche to prominence in the US. More recently he had suggested to Mercedes-Benz that if it produced a roadgoing version of its fabulous 'gullwing' 300SL racing car, he could sell a thousand of them. Now Hoffman suggested that what BMW needed to boost sales in the US was its own V8 sports car, and on top of that Hoffman suggested that the man to create the style of the car was Count Albrecht Goertz.

Born in Hanover, Goertz moved to America in 1937 and became a naturalized American, working as a garage mechanic while putting himself through a course in design at the renowned Pratt Institute. After working with Raymond Loewy on the design of Studebakers in the early 1950s, 'Al' Goertz set up in business for himself as a freelance designer, with offices on New York's East 57th Street, working on everything from watches to musical instruments.

Goertz designed two cars for BMW. The 503 was a two-door coupé or cabriolet based on the 502 chassis and running gear, with a 140bhp version of the V8 engine. Its styling was

Above: *Most 501 and 502 models were sedans (or 'limousines') but there were some coupés, like this 1954 502.*

Opposite center: *The 503 was no less handsome in coupé form. Goertz penned shapes which were far more modern than the conservative Munich-styled sedans.*

Opposite below: *High prices deterred 503 buyers, despite the car's fine looks. Just over 400 were sold before production ended in 1959.*

much cleaner and more modern than anything BMW had yet created itself, and the 503 was much admired. Even greater plaudits were in store for Goertz's other creation for BMW, the 507 sports car – though BMW preferred to call it a 'touring sports car.' Fitted with a 150bhp version of the 3.2-liter BMW V8 and capable of nearly 225km/h (140mph) given the right axle ratio, the 507 had the performance to justify its exotic looks. Goertz had flattened out the traditional BMW 'kidney' grille to give the 507 an aggressive twin-nostril front end, with a long hood and a fender line which gently dropped toward the rear of the car. The rear fender swelled upward from the back of the door to give the 507 a muscular, yet elegant, character. Behind each front wheel Goertz let a stylish vent into the fender, punctuated by a BMW roundel, and even the removable hard top, supplied as standard, integrated well. As a design it spoke well for Goertz's belief in 'the unity that makes for a work of art,' and that the best cars were designed by one person rather than by an army of designers, as was the case with America's domestic manufacturers. Goertz also railed against the acreage of chrome trim used by Detroit: 'Stamping right into the metal, which I consider more decorative, adds to the feeling of lightness and speed,' he told American magazine *Speed Age*. 'It's silly to waste money on fancy designs when simplicity will do the job and look more in keeping with the function of the car.' *Sports Car Illustrated* observed that it was 'that rare car which causes perfect strangers to stop and tell you how beautiful it is,' while many other commentators called this clean, classic design the most beautiful automotive shape they had ever seen.

But despite the plaudits it acquired for its Goertz styling, the 507 was hardly likely to pull BMW out of its increasingly parlous financial state. Hoffman, always one to back up his

Above: The Goertz-designed 503 Cabriolet was a fine touring machine. The stylish, Italianate looks were backed up with smooth power from BMW's 3.2-liter V8.

Left: Count Albrecht Goertz was born in Hanover, but moved to America in the 1930s. As a freelance designer his work included the stylish 503 and 507 BMWs.

BMW 503

Production	1955-59
Engine	All-alloy 90-degree V8, 16 overhead valves
Bore x stroke	82mm x 75mm
Capacity	3168cc
Power	140hp at 4800rpm
Torque	159lbft at 3800rpm
Fuel system	Two twin-choke Zenith carburetors
Gearbox	Four-speed manual, single dry-plate clutch
Chassis/body	Steel chassis with box-section and tubular members, separate aluminum alloy body
Suspension	Front: double wishbone and torsion bars Rear: live axle and torsion bars
Brakes	Hydraulically-operated drums all round
Performance	Top speed: 118mph (190km/h) 0-62mph (0-100km/h): 12.5sec

ideas with big numbers, had told BMW that he'd order 2000 507s on condition that the purchase price would be 12,000 deutschmarks. When the true cost turned out to be around twice that amount, Hoffman declined to commit himself to more than a handful – even if *Road &Track* was happy to inform readers that the 507 was 'worth its price'. There was talk of replacing the costly hand-beaten aluminum body with a series-production steel shell, expected to cut the list price in America from $8988 in 1957 to around $5000. But it never happened, and instead the 507 remained a handsome, hand-made sports car for the super-rich: just 253 were built, the last few of them with new-fangled disc front brakes and price tags in the US in excess of $10,000. The 503 fared little better, just over 400 finding buyers by the time production ended in 1959.

Neither did the reflected glory from these high-profile 'hero cars' generate the expected improvement in the reputation – and more importantly the sales performance – of the mainstream sedans. Another attempt to add kudos to the aging sedans also ended in failure: German chancellor Konrad Adenauer tried out BMW's big 505 limousine, a longer and even plusher version of the 502, but decided to stick with his tried and trusted Mercedes-Benz 300. Such was his fondness for the big Mercedes that he insisted on using it for all official engagements, even abroad, and the 300 is still popularly known as the 'Adenauer Mercedes.' The 505, meanwhile, never progressed beyond the prototype stage.

Below: *Even more handsome than the 503, the 507 was BMW's rival to the Mercedes-Benz 300SL roadster.*

BMW's board recognized that the increasingly antiquated styling and the high prices of the 501 and 502 models meant that they would never sell in sufficient quantities to generate the sort of profits the company needed for future investment. What Munich needed was a popular, low-priced product that could keep the factory busy and earn much-needed deutschmarks. It was a repeat of the Eisenach story in the late 1920s, and the solution proved to be much the same: BMW found just the car it needed already in production.

Enter the Isetta

Renzo Rivolta's Milan-based company Iso had started out making refrigerators, then branched into scooters and three-wheeled utility vehicles. In 1953 Rivolta set about building a tiny car to lure impecunious Italians away from scooters. The Isetta was a clever design, just 89in (2260mm) long, with a characteristic 'bubble' shape that inspired the name of a whole new genre of cars. The was only one door, which extended across the entire front of the car and carried the top mounting of the steering column so that the column hinged out of the way when the door was opened. The wide-tracked front wheels were given independent suspension, while the rear was a little more rudimentary: a track of less than 2ft (610mm) meant that the Isetta could get away without a differential. The engine, a 236cc two-stroke twin, was mounted low down at the rear.

BMW bought the rights to the Isetta, Rivolta spending the money from this and a similar deal with Velam in France on turning Iso into a manufacturer of supercars with American V8 engines. In Munich the Isetta was fitted with the four-stroke 247cc single-cylinder engine from the R25 motorcycle, and the re-engineered BMW Isetta 'Motocoupe' made its debut at the 1955 Frankfurt motor show, a curious sight alongside the big V8 cars. The following year there was an Isetta 300 with a 297cc engine, and later in 1956 the Isetta body was revised with larger side windows. BMW made more than 161,000 Isettas in eight years, and a few thousand more were built under license from BMW in Britain, where they had single rear wheels to take advantage of the cheaper road tax applied to three-wheeled vehicles. The 'bubble car' fad had perhaps already peaked when the Suez Crisis of 1956 and the oil shortages in Europe that followed it set buyers in search of tiny economy cars once again, giving bubble cars a new lease of life.

Above: The 507's removable hard top suited the car's lines remarkably well. With or without a roof, it was unquestionably a strong style statement.

Above: With 150bhp available from a tuned 3.2-liter V8 engine, the 507 had performance to match its looks.

Above: The well-appointed interior of the 507 supported BMW's claim that it was a 'touring sports car.

BMW 507

Production	1955-59
Engine	All-alloy 90-degree V8, 16 overhead valves
Bore x stroke	82mm x 75mm
Capacity	3168cc
Power	150hp at 5000rpm
Torque	174lbft at 4000rpm
Fuel system	Two twin-choke Zenith carburetors
Gearbox	Four-speed manual, single dry-plate clutch
Chassis/body	Steel chassis with box-section and tubular members, separate aluminum body
Suspension	Front: double wishbone and torsion bars Rear: live axle and torsion bars
Brakes	Hydraulically-operated drums all round
Performance	Top speed: 129mph (207km/h)* 0-60mph (0-97km/h): 9sec*

depending on axle ratio

Right: The 507, another Goertz design, was universally admired – but few could afford to buy one of these thoroughbreds.

Above: Isettas were hugely popular machines in the 1950s, and some even found their way into competition. This example finished the Mille Miglia in 1955 – in 267th position.

Right: The single door on the front of the Isetta provided easy access to the cabin despite the car's diminutive size.

BMW Isetta

Production	1955-63
Engine	Single cylinder, two overhead valves, cast iron cylinder head.
Bore x stroke	68mm x 68mm
Capacity	247cc
Power	12bhp at 5800rpm
Torque	Not quoted
Fuel system	Single Bing carburetor
Gearbox	Four-speed manual, single dry-plate clutch
Chassis/body	Tubular steel chassis with steel body
Suspension	Front: trailing arms and coil springs Rear: leaf-sprung live axle
Brakes	Hydraulically operated drums all round
Performance	Top speed: approximately 56mph (90km/h)

Back in Munich, BMW could see that the appeal of the Isetta, like that of the Dixi 3/15 some years before, would quickly fade away once the buying public felt that it could afford something a little better. Mindful of the yawning gap in the range between the tiny Isetta economy car and the vast and profligate V8s, BMW set about developing machines to fill the void. What it really needed was a medium-sized sedan of around 1.5-liters capacity, mid-way between the 297cc Isetta and the V8s of 2.6 liters or more. But building a totally new car, with a totally new engine, was out of the question: BMW just didn't have enough money. Instead, it built on the technology available by producing a bigger version of the Isetta, called the 600.

For the 600, Willy Black drew up an extended version of the Isetta chassis with the rear wheels moved outward to provide space for two rear seats and a more conventional rear track. The rear wheels were suspended from semi-trailing arms, a novelty at the time and one which was to go on serving BMW for many years to come. Egg-shaped like the Isetta, the 600 shared the smaller car's single front door but added a side door for access to the rear of the cabin. Power came from a 585cc version of the long-running BMW boxer motorcycle engine, giving the 600 spritely enough performance to worry bigger machines when Alex von Falkenhausen took one rallying with his wife in the navigator's chair.

Though nearly 35,000 were built between 1957 and 1959, the 600 failed to live up to expectations because of its price (only a little less than a Volkswagen) and its Isetta-like styling. The comical shape of the Isetta (Germans called it 'the rolling egg') was excusable for an out-and-out economy car, even quite chic for a while, but as soon as buyers had the wherewithal to look beyond the bubble cars they wanted something resembling a real car, not an object that reminded them that they were only a step beyond the most basic machines. The 700 that BMW readied for production during 1959 would address that problem.

As the designation suggests, the 700 was given a bigger motor than the 600, this time a 697cc derivative of the boxer motorcycle engine, developing 30bhp. But BMW avoided its mistake with the styling of the 600 by installing the engine in a completely new body, designed by talented Italian stylist Giovanni Michelotti. The first version to go on sale, in August 1959, was a two-door coupé and by the end of the year a sedan with a higher rear roof line had been added to the range.

While Isettas, and then the 600 and 700, kept the production lines at Munich busy, BMW continued tinkering with the V8 range in an effort to stir up some sales. In 1957 the 503's 140bhp V8 was dropped into the old 502 sedan body to produce the 502 3.2 Super. The following year the 502 tag was dropped, the sedan range now consisting of the 2.6 and 2.6 Luxury (100bhp), the 3.2 (120bhp) and the 3.2 Super (140bhp). But sales remained in the doldrums. Sales of the smaller cars were still healthy, but their low prices meant little profit for the company coffers. Worse still, BMW's other revenue streams were failing them: motorcycle sales dropped as the economy improved, German buyers started thinking of Volkswagens rather than sidecars, and the US Army finally moved out and stopped paying BMW rent. Munich fell deeper and deeper into debt, and was forced to ask its banks and even the Bavarian state for aid. BMW's biggest shareholders started to wonder if they were ever likely to see a return on their investment.

The crisis came at the company's Annual General Meeting in December 1959, when BMW's major shareholders – including the Deutsche Bank – put forward a redevelopment plan for the company which amounted to a cut-price takeover by Daimler-Benz. But BMW's smaller shareholders were keen to see the Munich company remain independent, and under the astute leadership of Frankfurt lawyer Dr. Friedrich Mathern the takeover was successfully fought off. The loyalty of these small shareholders to BMW and its independence, and their robust rebuttal of a takeover, caught the attention of a new group of investors who would be instrumental in turning BMW's fortunes around.

Above: The BMW Isetta 600 was based on an extended Isetta chassis, and powered by a version of the 'boxer' motorcycle engine.

BMW 600

Production	1957-59
Engine	Flat twin, four overhead valves, cast iron cylinder heads.
Bore x stroke	74mm x 68mm
Capacity	585cc
Power	19.5bhp at 4000rpm
Torque	29lbft at 2500rpm
Fuel system	Single Solex carburetor
Gearbox	Four-speed manual, single dry-plate clutch
Chassis/body	Tubular steel chassis with steel body
Suspension	Front: trailing arms and coil springs Rear: semi-trailing arms and coil springs
Brakes	Hydraulically operated drums all round
Performance	Top speed: approximately 62mph (100km/h)

Left: The 600 had a large front door, like the Isetta, supplemented by a single side door which gave access to the rear seats.

RESCUE AND REVIVAL
1959-72

Previous pages: The '02 series spawned several variants, including a convertible.

BMW 700

Production	1959-65
Engine	Flat twin, four overhead valves, cast iron cylinder heads.
Bore x stroke	78mm x 73mm
Capacity	697cc
Power	30bhp at 5000rpm
Torque	37lbft at 3400rpm
Fuel system	Single Solex carburetor
Gearbox	Four-speed manual, single dry-plate clutch
Chassis/body	Tubular steel chassis with steel body
Suspension	Front: trailing arms and coil springs
	Rear: semi-trailing arms and coil springs
Brakes	Hydraulically operated drums all round
Performance	Top speed: approximately 75mph (121km/h)

MW'S SAVIOR was Herbert Quandt, a Bavarian financier. Together with his half-brother Harald, Quandt already had a stake in BMW (and in other parts of the German motor industry, including Daimler-Benz) and was convinced by the arguments put forward for BMW's continued independence. With the powerful Quandt family backing BMW, the takeover that had been proposed by some members of the board was avoided and the Munich company enjoyed, at least, a stay of execution. But BMW still desperately needed new models to get itself back on its feet, and Quandt's first task was to put in place a fresh management team to deliver those new models.

The 700 was already proving an encouraging start on the road to BMW's recovery. The little coupé and the sedan which soon followed it found a ready market thanks to their Italianate good looks and spritely performance. In competition, too, the 700 quickly made its mark, though the car's debut race in March 1960 with Alex von Falkenhausen at the wheel ended in ignominy when the engine ingested a tiny rubber sealing ring from its own intake tract. Success followed soon after, with veteran Hans Stuck Sr. winning the German hillclimb championship in a 700 that year. The 700 picked up its first important class win at the Nürburgring six-hour touring car race in the hands of motorcycle champion Walter Schneider and Leo Levine. Works 700s picked up two more class wins at the Nürburgring that year, and at Hockenheim Stuck partnered Sepp Greger to a class win in the 12-hour race.

Rule changes for 1961 gave Falkenhausen and his team more freedom to modify the 700's engine. The road car's single carburetor gave way to a separate Amal carburetor for each cylinder, and with a revised camshaft and cylinder heads the 697cc engine gave up to 65bhp. Numerous class wins followed despite opposition from Abarth-modified Fiats and, in some races, the 1.3-liter Alfa Juniors. Even so, Schneider took the German sedan car title for 1961. Other notable racers competing in the 700 were Burkhard Bovensiepen (who later founded tuning company Alpina), Jacky Ickx (later a Formula 1 driver and multiple Le Mans winner),

Right: Veteran Hans Stuck Sr. took to the hills with the racing 700RS, with huge success.

Left: The 700 was a popular competition car, here squealing round a hairpin on the Monaco seafront during the 1961 Monte Carlo Rally.

and Hubert Hahne, who would quickly become a BMW works driver. BMW racing boss Alex von Falkenhausen could often be found behind the wheel, too.

While the 700 had been winning laurels on the race track, BMW's development engineers had been hard at work designing the new road cars that were so desperately needed. The first of those new models was the long-awaited mid-range sedan, first mooted back in the mid-1950s, which would help to fill the yawning gap in BMW's range between the Isetta and the 700 on one hand and the old V8-engined cars on the other. This 'Neue Klasse' or 'new range' car, the 1500, was shown to the public for the first time at the Frankfurt show in the fall of 1961 as a hastily-assembled prototype. Its crisp, square-rigged styling reflected that of the 700 but with an extra dose of maturity and functionality, while still retaining the attractive proportions of the smaller car. The shape was drawn in-house, though Michelotti – who had styled the 700 – was called in to add some finishing touches.

Below: BMW's Alex von Falkenhausen was a keen competitor, both in production-based cars and occasionally single seaters.

Like the styling, the running gear was new but with some similarities to BMW's previous practice. The rear suspension was a development of the semi-trailing arm system which had first been seen in the 600 and also underpinned the 700, and which BMW would rely on for years to come. The same layout, incidentally, would also be adopted by many other manufacturers including Rolls-Royce, Ford, and the old enemy, Mercedes-Benz. At the front BMW raised some eyebrows with its choice of MacPherson strut suspension, which is

Right: The 700's clean-cut Michelotti lines were one its major strengths. The cabriolet was particularly neat.

Right: The 700 Coupé was no less attractive.

Opposite: Though the 1500 was announced early in 1961, deliveries did not begin until October 1962.

cheaper than a double-wishbone set-up but offers many of the same advantages. Disc brakes were provided at the front.

A brand new engine powered this brand new car. Alex von Falkenhausen and his team had already drawn up several overhead-cam, four-cylinder engine designs of up to 1100cc as potential replacements for the flat-twin engine in the 700. With one eye on Alfa Romeo's strong, powerful four-cylinder engines with their five-bearing crankshafts and twin overhead camshafts, Falkenhausen proposed that the new engine should have a five-bearing crank for reliability and should eschew then-common pushrod overhead-valve design in favor of a single overhead camshaft, with the valves operated by rockers. This tended to produce a tall engine, but BMW kept the hood line of the new car low by canting over the engine at 30 degrees to the vertical. The block was designed for exceptional strength and stiffness to ensure that the engine was smooth and reliable, the block casting extending well beyond the crankshaft centerline. With a 71mm stroke and 82mm bore, the new engine displaced 1499cc, though Falkenhausen deliberately ensured there was plenty of room in the block for bigger bore and stroke dimensions to be introduced later. In its original form it produced a handy 75bhp, and a late increase in compression ratio boosted this to 80bhp before production began.

But that didn't happen for some time. Everyone at Munich realized that the new car was make or break for BMW, and they had pulled out all the stops to get the prototype 1500 ready for the Frankfurt show in 1961 in order to drum up some orders. Their efforts were rewarded by the positive reaction of press and public, and soon BMW had hundreds of deposits from expectant customers. But putting this far-from-ready car into production was another matter, and like the 501 of a decade earlier it was to be another year before customers started to take delivery of their cars. By then BMW had 20,000 orders to fulfill.

The 1500 finally started to roll out in October 1962. That same year the final development of the V8 cars was announced, in the form of the 3200CS coupé – styled by Bertone, and powered by a 160bhp version of the BMW V8 engine. Though only 538 were built between 1962 and the end of production in 1965 – by which time all the V8-powered cars had finally been dropped from BMW's range – the 3200CS would be important because of the influence its styling would have on another generation of BMW coupés to follow later in the 1960s.

End of the Isetta

At the other end of Munich's range the popular but barely profitable Isetta-based cars were also dropped to make way for more Neue Klasse production. The Isetta's production run ended in 1963 after more than 161,000 had been made, while the 700 (which had been augmented in 1962 by a long-wheelbase 'LS' version) came to an end in 1965 after nearly 190,000 had been built. Thereafter BMW pinned its hopes on the runaway success of the Neue Klasse cars, which were already driving BMW toward financial security. In 1963, for the first time in 20 years, Munich's directors could recommend paying a dividend to the shareholders, and the following year there was another, bigger payment. Production continued to rise and profits rose with them.

Ironically, while the quality of BMW's engineering had never been in doubt even when its range of cars had seemed ill-suited to the prevailing market conditions, now that Munich was building the right kind of cars, its technical superiority seemed to be wavering. The

BMW 1500	
Production	1962-64
Engine	In-line four cylinder, single overhead camshaft, eight valves, aluminum alloy cylinder head
Bore x stroke	82mm x 71mm
Capacity	1499cc
Power	80bhp at 5700rpm
Torque	87lbft at 3000rpm
Fuel system	Single Solex carburetor
Gearbox	Four-speed manual, single dry-plate clutch
Chassis/body	Unitary steel chassis/body
Suspension	Front: MacPherson struts Rear: semi-trailing arms and coil springs
Brakes	Hydraulically operated, disc front/drums rear
Performance	Top speed: approximately 93mph (150km/h)

Opposite: The rare 3200CS was the final development of the V8 line that had begun with the 502 in 1954.

Right: Italian styling house Bertone penned the 3200CS, and its shape would influence later BMW coupés.

Below right: A cabriolet 3200CS was built for Herbert Quandt.

Below : The V8-engined cars soldiered on until 1965.

hastily-designed 1500 proved to be less than bullet-proof: in service the mounting points for the rear semi-trailing suspension arms would sometimes separate from the body, the rear axle was prone to failure and the new all-synchromesh gearbox also gave problems. The 1500 lasted only until the end of 1964, when it was replaced by a much more thoroughly developed 1600, with a bored-out version of the same engine displacing 1573cc.

By then the original Neue Klasse sedan had been joined by a higher-performance derivative, the 1800, which carried only a little extra chrome trim and revised badging to differentiate it externally from its sister car. The 90bhp, 1773cc engine shared its 84mm bore

with the 1600 but had a longer 80mm stroke, and the extra power turned the Neue Klasse into a 100mph (161km/h) car. Soon after, an even quicker version was added, the 109mph (175km/h) 1800TI (for 'Touring International'). The TI engine was fitted with a pair of twin-choke Solex carburetors and developed 110bhp, and thus equipped the car could despatch the benchmark 0-60mph (0-97km/h) sprint in a fraction over 11 seconds. It provided sports car performance in a comfortable, practical sedan, and gave BMW a machine which could hold its own in production sedan car racing – once Alex von Falkenhausen's men had given it some apparently very minor tweaks which resulted in an output of no less than 160bhp. The bigger engine capacity also helped by putting the racing 1800TI into a different capacity class to the very fast 1.6-liter Lotus-Cortinas and Alfa Romeo Giulias. That 1964 season saw the 1800TI record its class win and seventh overall in the Nürburgring 6-hours (Hubert Hahne driving with Swiss Anton Fischhaber), and Hahne partnered Heinrich Eppelein to an overall win in the Nürburgring 12-hours the following month. An even longer race followed, the Spa 24-hours, where BMW entered two 1800TIs – Eppelein was partnered by Walter Schneider, while Hahne shared with the 'Flying Finn,' rally driver Rauno Aaltonen. Despite stopping to change wheel bearings the Hahne/Aaltonen car finished second overall to the Mercedes-Benz 300SE of Robert Crevits and Gustave Gosselin. Outright wins in European Touring Car Championship events soon followed, with Hahne winning at Zandvoort and then again in the Budapest Grand Prix, to finish the year as German Saloon Car Champion.

The Lotus-Cortina had introduced a new science to sedan car racing, that of the 'homologation special' – a special version of a production sedan built in just sufficient numbers to qualify for a production racing category, and with modifications designed with racing use in mind. By the mid-1970s the use of homologation specials to build racing and rally cars would be almost universal, but in the early 1960s it was practically unheard of.

BMW 3200CS

Production	1962-65
Engine	All-alloy 90 degree V8, 16 overhead valves
Bore x stroke	82mm x 75mm
Capacity	3169cc
Power	160bhp at 5600rpm
Torque	177lbft at 3600rpm
Fuel system	Two Zenith carburetors
Gearbox	Four-speed manual, single dry-plate clutch
Chassis/body	Tubular steel chassis with steel body
Suspension	Front: wishbones and torsion bars Rear: live axle with torsion bars
Brakes	Hydraulically operated, disc front/drums rear
Performance	Top speed: approximately 124mph (200km/h) 0-62mph (0-100km/h): 14sec

Above: Some 'Neue Klasse' sedans still compete today in historic racing.

Right: Hubert Hahne conducting a racing 1800TI in typically exuberant style. Hahne won the German championship in 1964.

BMW 1800TI

Production	1964–66
Engine	In-line four cylinder, single overhead camshaft, eight valves, aluminum alloy cylinder head
Bore x stroke	84mm x 80mm
Capacity	1773cc
Power	110bhp at 5800rpm
Torque	111lbft at 4000rpm
Fuel system	Two twin-choke Solex carburetors
Gearbox	Four-speed manual, single dry-plate clutch
Chassis/body	Unitary steel chassis/body
Suspension	Front: MacPherson struts Rear: semi-trailing arms and coil springs
Brakes	Hydraulically operated, disc front/drums rear
Performance	Top speed: approximately 109mph (175km/h) 0–60mph (0–97km/h): approximately 11sec

Developed by Lotus from the humdrum Ford Cortina family sedan, the Lotus-Cortina shared its hand-built twin-overhead-cam engine with the Lotus Elan sports car and benefited from the suspension design genius of Lotus boss Colin Chapman. Very rapid in 1964, the Lotus-Cortina then swept the board in 1965's European Touring Car Championship with Sir John Whitmore's Alan Mann-prepared car winning all but one round. BMW, meanwhile, had created a homologation special of its own, the 1800TI/SA ('SA' standing for *Sonderausführung* or 'special equipment'). Included in the specification was a tuned engine with big Weber carburetors instead of the twin-choke Solexes of the plain 1800TI, helping the 1800TI/SA road car develop more than 150bhp and boosting the race-prepared machines to around 165bhp. A five-speed Getrag gearbox was also fitted, and there were wider wheels and anti-roll bars front and rear to improve cornering, despite which the car had been pared down to a running weight 44lb (20kg) lighter than the 1800TI. The race cars, with minimal trim and lightweight panels, were even lighter. Even this wasn't enough against the Lotus-Cortinas, though BMW salvaged some pride with an overall win at the Spa 24-hours when the Lotus-Cortinas stayed at home.

New coupé

The summer of 1965 had seen a new addition to BMW's engine range, a 1990cc unit which shared the 80mm stroke of the existing 1800 engine but had been bored out to 89mm. Instead of dropping the expanded motor into the sedan shell straight away, BMW instead introduced it in a new coupé body which combined elements of the recently-departed, Bertone-styled 3200CS coupé and the Michelotti-influenced Neue Klasse sedan. Despite its mixed parentage, the package turned out to work rather well, its imposing front end with four headlamps faired-in behind glass covers being rather tidier than the Bertone body's fussy nose. Bodies for the coupés were built by Karmann, which had made its name building the Volkswagen 'Beetle' cabriolet and the Beetle-derived Karmann Ghia sports coupés. The new coupé was available in two forms, as a 2000C (for 'Coupé') with a single carburetor, 100bhp engine or a 2000CS ('Coupé Sport') with twin Solexes and 120bhp.

The 2.0-liter engine, in its single- and twin-carb forms, went into the sedan in January 1966 to produce the 2000 and 2000TI. In a road test headlined 'Everything just right' Britain's *Motor* magazine pointed out that the 2000TI was more economical than the 1800, while offering better acceleration than rivals like the Alfa Giulia TI and even sprinting quicker than such sporting machinery as Triumph's TR4A and the Mercedes-Benz 230SL. The TI took over as BMW's front-line racing machine from July, helping Hahne to the European Touring Car

BMW 2000CS	
Production	1965-69
Engine	In-line four cylinder, single overhead camshaft, eight valves, aluminum alloy cylinder head
Bore x stroke	89mm x 80mm
Capacity	1990cc
Power	120bhp at 5500rpm
Torque	123lbft at 3600rpm
Fuel system	Two twin-choke Solex carburetors
Gearbox	Four-speed manual, single dry-plate clutch
Chassis/body	Unitary steel chassis/body
Suspension	Front: MacPherson struts Rear: semi-trailing arms and coil springs
Brakes	Hydraulically operated, disc front/drums rear
Performance	Top speed: approximately 110mph (177km/h) 0-60mph (0-97km/h): 10.4sec

Above left: The 1600-2 was the first of the two-door cars based on the Neue Klasse.

Left: A 2.0-liter engine went into the Neue Klasse sedans in 1966 to produce the 2000 and 2000TI.

Opposite: Stuttgart coachbuilder Baur built convertible '02s in comparatively small numbers in the late 1960s.

Left: The 2000 Touring had the added practicality of a 'hatchback' body.

Championship title that year despite the emergence of the lightweight Alfa GTAs in the 1.6-liter class. Nine Alfas turned up for the Spa 24-hours that year, but even so BMW won it for the second consecutive year with a 2000TI driven by Hahne and Jacky Ickx at an average speed of nearly 105mph (169km/h).

The Geneva show of March 1966 saw BMW follow up the Neue Klasse four-door sedans and the 2000C/CS coupés with a new model, the 1600-2. The '1600' part of the designation signified use of the 1573cc engine from the 1600 sedan, production of which would soon end, while the '2' indicated that this new car had two doors. The shorter two-door shell was around 286lb (130kg) lighter than the four-door, and the shorter wheelbase made the 1600-2 a more wieldy car to handle in tight bends. To many eyes it was better proportioned than the sedan on which it was based and it was cheaper to make, too, which meant that BMW could offer it at a comparatively low price. On the one hand this gave Munich an additional range to cater for those who couldn't quite afford the four-door Neue Klasse sedan, and on the other it produced a credible rival for some of Alfa Romeo's two-door, four-seat coupés. BMW took the fight to the Milanese marque still further the following year with the introduction of a twin-carb version simply called the 1600TI.

Apfelbeck and F2

Though the lighter two-door cars looked like obvious candidates for touring car racing, there were no works entries in international sedan car racing in 1967. Instead BMW concentrated on building engines for single-seater racing formulae, using the production four-cylinder block fitted with a new cylinder head with four valves per cylinder. Ludwig Apfelbeck, who had previously worked on four-valve cylinder heads for KTM motorcycles, built a single-cylinder 500cc test engine which developed 54bhp, proving the potential of a new valve layout which Apfelbeck favored. Conventional multi-valve engines had valves in pairs, either side of a 'pent roof' combustion chamber, with the inlet valves on one side and the exhaust valves on the other. This kept the plumbing neat, with the exhaust manifold on one side of the engine and the carburetors or fuel injection system on the other side. Apfelbeck's design was very different, with all four valves facing directly outward in opposed pairs. Think of each cylinder as a clock face with 12 at the front of the engine: the Apfelbeck head

BMW 1600-2	
Production	1966-71 (1971-75 badged as 1602)
Engine	In-line four cylinder, single overhead camshaft, eight valves, aluminum alloy cylinder head
Bore x stroke	84mm x 71mm
Capacity	1573cc
Power	83bhp at 5700rpm
Torque	96lbft at 3500rpm
Fuel system	Single Solex carburetor
Gearbox	Four-speed manual, single dry-plate clutch
Chassis/body	Unitary steel chassis/body
Suspension	Front: MacPherson struts Rear: semi-trailing arms and coil springs
Brakes	Hydraulically operated, disc front/drums rear
Performance	Top speed: approximately 99mph (159km/h) 0-60mph (0-97km/h): approx 11.5sec

had inlet valves at one o'clock and seven o'clock, with exhaust valves at four o'clock and ten o'clock. One of the advantages was that a potentially more efficient hemispherical combustion chamber could be used, but there were problems. Once the Apfelbeck design had been adapted for a 2.0-liter four-cylinder in-line engine, there were eight vertical intake ports, each with its own carburetor, and eight exhaust pipes. It made for a tall and cluttered motor, and was later branded the 'high and heavy' engine. Hahne and Falkenhausen brought an old Brabham Formula 1 chassis back from England and installed the new engine, Hahne taking the wheel for the car's debut at an Austrian hillclimb in 1966, which it won. The car reappeared later that year running on nitromethane racing fuel at Hockenheim, where Falkenhausen and Hahne set a batch of standing-start records despite the drivers worrying about all those carburetors spitting back: nitromethane is very explosive...

That record-breaking engine developed around 330bhp and even running on normal gasoline the 2.0-liter Apfelbeck punched out 260bhp, proving that there was potential in the design. For 1967 BMW produced a version for Formula 2, which required 1.6-liter production-based engines, in which form the Apfelbeck engine produced 225bhp – encouragingly, a little more than the rival Ford-based Cosworth FVA engine. Four BMW-powered Lolas were prepared, two to be run by John Surtees in England and two more to be run from Munich, with drivers including Surtees, Hahne, Jo Siffert, Chris Irwin, and Andrea de Adamich. But the Apfelbeck engine was dogged by reliability problems, because its complex valve gear couldn't survive for long at the engine speeds required for a competitive power output - which meant 10,000rpm or more.

By now BMW's range of road cars had grown considerably, and it was producing more cars than ever – nearly 60,000 left Munich in 1965. That meant more production space was needed, and to make room for more motor cars the motorcycle production lines were progressively moved to Berlin. More capacity came in 1967 when the Bavarian state asked BMW to step in and save the troubled Glas company at Dingolfing, an hour's drive to the north-east of BMW's Munich base. Ironically, back in BMW's dark days in the 1950s Glas had been approached to see if it might want to take over the Munich firm...

Hans Glas started out making agricultural machinery, then diversified into scooters in 1951 and bubble cars, with the well-known Goggomobil, from 1955 to 1966. Mid-size sedans and expensive coupés were also built at Dingolfing, with the Maserati-like 'Glaserati,' the

Above: A tense-looking mechanic fires up the Apfelbeck-engined Brabham at Hockenheim in 1966. The nitromethane-fueled engine developed 330bhp.

Left: The Glas 1700GT was given a BMW engine and a rather unhappy BMW grille following Munich's takeover.

3000 V8, at the top of the range. BMW rebadged the Glas cars, and redeveloped them with BMW technology. The Goggomobil quickly bit the dust, and the smaller of the Glas coupés – the 1700GT – was given a 1.6-liter BMW engine and BMW semi-trailing arm rear suspension for its relaunch as the BMW 1600GT. The big V8 Glas coupé, with dubious Frua styling, soldiered on in small-scale production for a couple of years. Though BMW had bigger and bolder plans for the former Glas factory at Dingolfing, yet more additions to the growing range of BMW cars were to appear first.

The standards of luxury trim and equipment in BMW's cars continued to rise, with ZF three-speed automatic transmission becoming a popular option from 1966. In 1968 the 2000TI sedan was reinvented with a more luxurious interior as the 2000tilux. As BMW aimed its sights ever higher, thoughts turned to even more luxurious cars, bigger and with more powerful engines. Even though the four-cylinder engines had done a sterling job powering ever faster versions of the Neue Klasse

sedans, the drive toward greater power together with greater refinement directed BMW back toward engines with more cylinders. New six-cylinder engines appeared in September 1968, based closely on the existing in-line fours and available in two versions – a 2.5-liter with 150bhp and a 2.8-liter with 170bhp. From the launch the new sixes were available in two body styles, a revised version of the 2000CS coupé and a brand new big sedan.

Above: BMW kept the Glas 3000 V8 coupé in production for a while, but had big plans for the Dingolfing factory where it was made.

Above: The six-cylinder engines launched in 1968 were available in a new coupé body based on the 2000CS. This is the top-of-the-range 2800CS.

Known as the 2500 or 2800 depending on engine size, the new sedan took BMW back into a market that it had vacated back in 1964 with the demise of the old-school V8 sedans. It also propelled the Munich firm back into competition with its old adversary, Mercedes-Benz, which had launched a 'New Generation' mid-range sedan, the W114/115 series, in 1967. In many ways these new sedans were simply the Neue Klasse writ large, with similarly crisp body styling, six-cylinder engines based heavily on the older cars' in-line fours and similar all-independent suspension – again there were MacPherson struts at the front end and BMW's trademark semi-trailing arms at the rear. A front anti-roll bar was standard on the CS but optional on the sedans, though the fractionally heavier four-door cars featured an all-disc braking system while the 2800CS made do with drums on its rear axle.

Above: *The new sixes, in 2.5-liter and 2.8-liter capacities, were also available in the big E3 sedan. BMW was once again challenging Mercedes-Benz.*

Left: *The swift six-cylinder cars soon found their way into competition. Circuit racing was a natural home, but here a 2800 tackles the Monte Carlo Rally.*

In that same year, 1968, BMW introduced another variation on the Neue Klasse theme. Alex von Falkenhausen had dropped a 2.0-liter engine into a 1600-2 for his own use, and it turned out that BMW director Helmut Werner Bonsch had independently done exactly the same thing. The two men agreed that a 2.0-liter two-door was a saleable proposition, and persuaded the BMW board to put the car into production as the 2002. It provided all the all-out performance of the 1600TI, together with considerably better flexibility thanks to its beefier low-rev torque. The 2002 also presented BMW with a performance sedan for the American market, which had been denied the 1600TI because its twin-carburetor engine could not pass the increasingly stringent US exhaust emissions tests. Inevitably the same problem meant that American BMW enthusiasts were unable to buy the twin-carburetor 2002TI which was made available in some markets, offering still greater levels of performance thanks to its 120bhp engine fed by twin Solexes. British BMW enthusiasts were denied the 2002TI, too, because the car was only built with left-hand drive.

Racing the 2002TI

The 2002TI was an obvious candidate for touring car racing, and a BMW works team was lined up alongside the latest BMW cars for international F2 racing. The latest version of the F2 engine had abandoned the Apfelbeck head for a new design, the 'Diametral.' Now the four valves in each cylinder were arranged in pairs either side of the combustion chamber with the stems of each pair parallel (as in more conventional four-valve layouts) but still there was an inlet and an exhaust valve on each side. The inlet valves were positioned at ten o'clock and four o'clock, with the exhaust valves at two o'clock and eight o'clock. Because the valves were arranged in straight rows along each side of the engine, the valve gear was

BMW 2800	
Production	1968-76
Engine	In-line four cylinder, single overhead camshaft, eight valves, aluminum alloy cylinder head
Bore x stroke	86mm x 80mm
Capacity	2788cc
Power	170bhp at 6000rpm
Torque	174lbft at 3700rpm
Fuel system	Two Zenith carburetors
Gearbox	Four-speed manual, single dry-plate clutch
Chassis/body	Unitary steel chassis/body
Suspension	Front: MacPherson struts Rear: semi-trailing arms and coil springs
Brakes	Hydraulically operated discs all round
Performance	Top speed: 128mph (206km/h) 0-60mph (0-97km/h): 8.5sec

much simpler than before and could be expected to offer greater reliability. The plumbing was still a nightmare, however, with eight separate intake trumpets for the Kugelfischer mechanical fuel injection, eight injectors, and eight exhaust primary pipes arranged in two groups of four. The Diametral design also called for no less than three spark plugs *per cylinder*. Peak power was slightly down compared to the Apfelbeck engine, but still fractionally better than the 215bhp quoted for the F2 Cosworth FVA. Even so, the Lola-BMW combination failed to make much headway, though it could at least be expected to finish races.

Formula 2 promise

There was more hope early in 1969 when Hahne finished a scant 0.6 seconds behind the Matra-Cosworth of Jean-Pierre Beltoise at Hockenheim. Later in the season the F2 Lolas were replaced by a new car called the BMW 269, designed by English engineer Len Terry and built by the Dornier aircraft factory. Hahne finished second in the European F2 championship, but it was not a happy season for BMW's F2 team: a practice crash in Sicily left Hahne with a broken foot, and worse was to come that summer, when former hillclimb champion Gerhard Mitter was killed at the Nürburgring after crashing at Flugplatz. That was to lead more than a year later to the end of BMW factory involvement in single-seater racing. By this time the experiments with curious valve layouts had been abandoned and the F2 engine had a acquired a more conventional parallel valve engine with paired intake and exhaust valves. Even after the factory pulled out, a band of loyal engineers including Falkenhausen and engine man Paul Rosche continued to operate out of a tiny private workshop, running a BMW-powered March in F2 with Dieter Quester at the helm, with some success.

The 2002TI had joined the fray back in 1968, the earliest racing versions running 200bhp carburetored engines. Soon F2-style Kugelfischer fuel injection was part of the racing sedan spec, and the 2002s proved to be far more successful than BMW's F2 venture. Despite

BMW 2002tii	
Production	1969-75
Engine	In-line four cylinder, single overhead camshaft, eight valves, aluminum alloy cylinder head
Bore x stroke	89mm x 80mm
Capacity	1990cc
Power	130bhp at 5800rpm
Torque	131lbft at 4500rpm
Fuel system	Kugelfischer mechanical fuel injection
Gearbox	Four-speed manual, single dry-plate clutch
Chassis/body	Unitary steel chassis/body
Suspension	Front: MacPherson struts Rear: semi-trailing arms and coil springs
Brakes	Hydraulically operated, disc front/drums rear
Performance	Top speed: approximately 113mph (182km/h) 0-60mph (0-97km/h): 8.2sec

Above: For rallying the 2002s carried a battery of auxiliary lamps in front of the radiator grille.

Right: Achim Warmbold and Jean Todt won the 1973 Austrian Alpine Rally but were disqualified on a technicality. Warmbold was the last BMW works rally driver.

*Above:*The 2002 Turbo delighted enthusiasts and infuriated the road safety lobby. The reversed script on the air dam – designed to read correctly in the rear-view mirror of the driver in front – was removed.

Above left: By 1968, when this 2002 was built, the car was firmly established as an enthusiast's favorite.

Above: The 2002 Turbo engine provided a massive leap in power compared to the 2002tii – but at some cost. 'Turbo lag' was considerable, and it needed a committed and skillful driver to get the best out of it.

Left: The 2002 Turbo was introduced to help inject new life into the range. It would have succeeded, but for the 'Yom Kippur' oil crisis.

Variations on a theme: '02 Touring, Cabriolet, and Targa

THE '02-SERIES, as the two-door cars were known, were not only available as fixed-roof sedans – they came in three other guises during their production life. The first, from 1968, was the work of Stuttgart coachbuilder Baur, which developed a Cabriolet version available with either a 1.6-liter or 2.0-liter engine. Nothing projected above the waistline except the windshield and its frame, which made for exceptionally clean and elegant looks, but by the early 1970s there was more concern about passenger safety in accidents. Baur replaced the Cabriolet cars with a 2002 Targa, which incorporated a fixed roll-over bar behind the front passengers' heads. A removable roof panel was provided for the front part of the roof and there was a drop-down rear section, allowing several different fresh-air options. All the open-top cars were built in very small numbers.

Also rare is the Touring, a three-door hatchback version of the '02 introduced in 1971. Engines ranged right up to the 2002tii unit, in which form the Touring anticipated the development of the 'hot hatch,' popularized by cars like the Volkswagen Golf GTI in the late 1970s. Sadly the Touring was ahead of its time and buyers didn't quite know what to make of it, so sales were low.

Right: The '02-series two-door sedan was the first of a family of small BMWs, and by far the most common variant.

Below: Baur built two different convertibles, the second version with a fixed roll-over hoop for extra accident protection.

UNBEATABLE
BMW
1972-80

Previous pages: The be-winged racing CSL
fought a titanic battle with Ford in the 1973
European Touring Car Championship.

Above: *The new BMW headquarters building
under construction. The 'four-cylinder' was
built near the site of the original BMW factory.*

AULED BACK from the very brink of bankruptcy by Herbert Quandt's faith and
by impressive new products beginning with the giant-killing 700, BMW had gone
from strength to strength in the 1960s. Now the city of Munich prepared for the
1972 Olympic Games, constructing a brand new Olympic Village on what had once been the
Oberwiesenfeld airfield – where the original Bayerische Motoren Werke and Bayerische
Flugzeug Werke had set up shop 60 years earlier. For BMW it was also a period of
construction, with its brand new 'four cylinder' headquarters going up alongside the
Olympic Village in Munich, close to the location of that original factory. BMW was also
building a new production hall at the Dingolfing plant that it had inherited from Glas in
1967. It was here that a vital new range of cars would be built.

By now BMW had an impressive range of attractive, quality cars, each one of which could
compete on level terms with its in-class rivals. In 1972 BMW would go one better, producing
a brand new car which, some would argue, was not just competitive in its class but one
which redefined the boundaries of its type and changed the perceptions of a whole
generation of car buyers. As if that wasn't enough, it also kicked off a new numbering
system which would mark out BMW cars for generations to come.

That car was the 5-series – so-called, some said, because it was the fifth different line of
cars since the watershed of 1959. It was a mid-range sedan car that began where the now
ageing Neue Klasse cars left off. Like those four-door sedans, the 5-series was initially
powered by four-cylinder engines, starting with the 2.0-liter four from the 2000. Fitted with
twin Stromberg carburetors in the BMW 520, the 2.0-liter engine was good for 115bhp. The
5-series also shared its basic suspension layout with the Neue Klasse cars, with MacPherson
struts at the front and a trailing arm rear end which was by now universal in Munich's
products. There were similarities about the styling too, with clean-cut lines and generous
glazing, but there was no mistaking that this was a brand new car. Bigger all round (it was,
in fact, only a little shorter than the E3 2500/2800) it offered much better accommodation for
drivers and passengers than before.

Turbo concept

Safety, too, was much improved. Ralph Nader's influential book *Unsafe At Any Speed* had
brought to public notice what he called the 'designed-in dangers' of American automobiles,
and further weight was lent to the argument when American insurance companies raised
their premiums, tired of the welter of claims from drivers of fast but evil-handling 'muscle
cars.' As a result, at the beginning of the 1970s many manufacturers placed a much greater
emphasis on safety and on keeping repair costs low. In 1972 BMW showcased the fruits of its
safety research in a mid-engined supercar concept called, simply, the BMW Turbo. In
addition to a 200bhp, turbocharged 2002 engine and 155mph (250km/h) performance, the
Turbo included such innovations as a radar system to warn the driver of inadequate braking
distance to the car ahead, crushable foam-filled front and rear sections replacing
conventional bumpers, and side impact beams – all of which would return on production
cars in future years.

The 5-series incorporated the 'safety cell' concept which had been pioneered by
Mercedes-Benz in the 1950s, but it also paid attention to 'primary safety' – the ability to
avoid an accident in the first place. Roadholding and braking were first class, as was

Above: The first-generation 5-series was designed with safety in mind, reflecting the public concerns of the era.

Left: The Turbo concept of 1972 in front of the BMW headquarters. Munich was justifiably proud of both.

BMW 520

Production	1972-81
Engine	In-line four-cylinder, single overhead camshaft, eight valves, aluminum alloy cylinder head
Bore x stroke	89mm x 80mm
Capacity	1991cc
Power	113bhp at 5800rpm
Torque	122lbft at 3700rpm
Fuel system	Stromberg carburetor
Gearbox	Four-speed manual, single dry-plate clutch
Chassis/body	Unitary steel chassis/body
Suspension	Front: MacPherson struts Rear: semi-trailing arms and coil springs
Brakes	Hydraulically operated, disc front, drum rear
Performance	Top speed: 107mph (172km/h) 0-60mph (0-97km/h): 12.0sec

expected of any BMW. There was another subtler element to the car's safety provisions inside: the dashboard and control layouts had been ergonomically designed to make operating the car a simpler, more intuitive process. Again, it was a theme which would reappear in the future, being a widely admired feature of all BMWs from then on.

While the 5-series took BMW's road cars into a whole new era, the company's racing activities were also undergoing major changes. Alpina's racing efforts had begun to focus on the big six-cylinder BMW coupés in 1969, when Nicholas Koob and Helmut Kelleners took a mildy-modified 2800CS to ninth place in the Spa 24-hour race. By 1970 Alpina had made enough progress with the car to win two events outright, Alex Soler Roig taking the checkered flag at the Salzburgring and Kelleners returning to Spa with Austrian Gunther Huber to win the 24-hour event.

BMW retired from racing as a works team at the end of 1970, but continued with a sporadic rally program which had begun in 1969, and which would later yield some small rewards in the hands of Bjorn Waldegaard and Achim Warmbold (whose navigator was Jean Todt, today Managing Director of Ferrari). The Munich roundel also appeared on racing machines entered under privateer flags. Dieter Quester's Formula 2 program for 1971 with a March 712 chassis was provided with 'crossflow' BMW engines by 'BMW Underground Racing,' the out-of-hours operation led by Falkenhausen. Quester won the usual slipstreaming contest at the high-speed Monza track and finished second five times, to end the year third in the championship behind Ronnie Peterson and Carlos Reutemann. That was the final year of the 1.6-liter regulations in European Formula 2, and BMW did not yet have a competitive unit that qualified for the upcoming 2.0-liter 'production based' F2. Instead a 2.0-liter version of the old F2 engine was installed in a Chevron sports car, which turned in some promising performances during 1972.

Below: A 2.5-liter version of the 'big six' engine went into the 5-series in 1973 to produce the 525.

Left: Dieter Quester and Toine Hezemans won the Spa 24-hours in 1973 in this works 3.3-liter CSL.

couple of days in a wind tunnel with a racing CSL trying a variety of aerodynamic aids, until a package was found which negated the lift and even generated a small amount of downforce. A production version was quickly created and applied to the CSL, which now gained a bigger front air dam, 'splitters' along the tops of the front fenders, and a hoop above the rear window directing air to a wing mounted on tall pedestals either side of the trunk lid. A new long-stroke 3.2-liter engine was also added, though the car was still known as a 3.0CSL. This revised car was homologated on July 1, 1973, and a week later the racing version appeared at the Nürburgring, where tests had already shown that the new wing system was worth 15 seconds a lap. Lauda's Alpina car proved to be the quickest and led until suspension problems dropped it down the order, but the Alpina CSL still finished third behind the two works CSLs, Stuck/Amon a lap ahead of Hezemans/Quester. The best Ford was the fifth-placed privateer Capri of Karl-Ludwig Weiss and Klaus Ludwig, the works cars having succumbed to a variety of failures and accidents.

Tragic races

BMW won again at Spa two weeks later, the Hezemans/Quester works CSL heading the Mass/Fitzpatrick Capri at the end of a tragic race, in which a freak collision claimed the lives of Hans-Peter Joisten in one of the two Alpina CSLs and Frenchman Roger Dubos in an Autodelta Alfa GTV. Alpina withdrew its second CSL, and after Autodelta's Massimo Larini was hurt in another accident Autodelta withdrew its remaining cars. Larini later died from his injuries.

The atmosphere was hardly any better when the European Touring Car Championship contenders gathered for the sixth round of the series, at Zandvoort in Holland. Two weeks earlier, in the Dutch Grand Prix, the promising and personable young Briton Roger Williamson had crashed his March after what appeared to be a tire failure. The car overturned and caught fire, but the race was not stopped – so the fire crews stationed further round the lap, unable to drive against the oncoming race traffic, could do nothing but watch

BMW 3.0CSL (ETCC)

Racing season	1974
Engine	In-line six-cylinder, twin overhead camshafts, 24 valves, aluminum alloy cylinder head
Bore x stroke	94mm x 84mm
Capacity	3498cc
Power	440bhp at 8500rpm
Torque	Not quoted
Fuel system	Kugelfischer mechanical fuel injection
Gearbox	Getrag five-speed manual, single dry-plate clutch
Chassis/body	Unitary steel chassis/body with aluminum alloy outer panels, glassfiber wheel arch extensions and aerodynamic package
Suspension	Front: MacPherson struts Rear: semi-trailing arms and coil springs
Brakes	Hydraulically operated, discs all round, four-piston front calipers
Performance	Top speed: approximately 170mph (274km/h)* 0-60mph (0-97km/h): 4.0sec*

* depending on gearing

Above: Hans-Joachim Stuck in the BMW-powered F2 March.

Right: Hans Stuck Senior and his son Hans-Joachim – both highly successful drivers of BMW competition machinery.

Opposite top: BMW's big coupés were elegant and powerful, with an enviable competition record. This is a 3.0CSi.

Opposite below: The 3-series was introduced in 1975 to replace the aging '02 models.

the cloud of smoke rising from beyond the trees. Another March driver, David Purley, stopped and fought in vain to pull Williamson from the burning car (he was later awarded a George Medal for his bravery). For F1, it was to be a season of tragedies and near-tragedies, culminating in the loss of François Cevert at Watkins Glen in October.

Safety at Zandvoort

For the Zandvoort Trophy touring car race the organizers drafted in rescue cars from Germany to supplement the inadequate safety provisions at the circuit. The works CSLs now sported their full 3.5-liter engines on a twisty circuit where engine output was more important than the BMW's new-found aerodynamic superiority, and holes now peppered the front spoilers of the CSLs to admit cooling air to the BMW's overheating front tires. Hezemans and Quester shared one works CSL as usual, with the other in the hands of Stuck and Tecno F1 driver Chris Amon, the two works cars lined up on the front row of the grid with the Capri of Jochen Mass/Dieter Glemser. At the start Hezemans and Stuck in the BMWs contested the lead with the Mass Capri, as Pescarolo kept in touch in the Schnitzer CSL. But the intense pace took its toll: a privateer Capri retired, and one of the works cars pitted with minor engine trouble. Stuck brought in his CSL after a trip into the sand trap, and soon after the car retired with gearbox trouble. The Mass Capri went out too, with a broken half-shaft, and the Ertl/Pescarolo Schnitzer BMW stopped to replace a worn tire. The result was another win for the Hezemans/Quester works CSL, followed home by the Alpina car of experienced sedan car racer Brian Muir and rising F1 star James Hunt, and the John Fitzpatrick/Gérard Larrousse Capri.

The Hezemans/Quester partnership won again in September at the Paul Ricard circuit in France, heading a train of CSLs – two works cars and two Alpinas. The best of the Capris was in the hands of Jochen Mass and Jackie Stewart; only a week later the Scot would clinch

BMW 633CSi

Production	1972-77
Engine	In-line six-cylinder, single overhead camshaft, 12 valves, aluminum alloy cylinder head
Bore x stroke	89mm x 86mm
Capacity	3210cc
Power	197bhp at 5500rpm
Torque	210lbft at 4250rpm
Fuel system	Bosch L-Jetronic fuel injection
Gearbox	Four-speed manual, single dry-plate clutch
Chassis/body	Unitary steel chassis/body
Suspension	Front: MacPherson struts Rear: semi-trailing arms and coil springs
Brakes	Hydraulically operated, discs all round
Performance	Top speed: 134mph (216km/h) 0-60mph (0-97km/h): 8.0sec

his third and final F1 World Championship in a Ford-engined Tyrrell. Cooling and fuel injection problems delayed them, and then the engine dropped a valve to leave the Capri struggling to the finish on five cylinders. Team mates Fitzpatrick and Larrousse in the other Capri broke an exhaust valve, and the damage was terminal – not just to the RS2600, but also to Ford's hopes of retaining the European Championship.

The final round of the championship was at Silverstone in September for the RAC Tourist Trophy, held over two two-hour heats. Schnitzer was absent, but there were two works CSLs and two Alpina cars, alongside three Cologne Capris and some quick British championship cars. The BMWs were quickest in practice, led by Stuck's works car ahead of Frank Gardner's well-known SCA Freight Camaro. Handling problems on the high-speed

BMW 316 E21

Production	1975-77
Engine	In-line four-cylinder, single overhead camshaft, eight valves, aluminum alloy cylinder head
Bore x stroke	84mm x 71mm
Capacity	1574cc
Power	90bhp at 6000rpm
Torque	90lbft at 4000rpm
Fuel system	Solex carburetor
Gearbox	Four-speed manual, single dry-plate clutch
Chassis/body	Unitary steel chassis/body
Suspension	Front: MacPherson struts Rear: semi-trailing arms and coil springs
Brakes	Hydraulically operated, disc front, drum rear
Performance	Top speed: approximately 99mph (160km/h) 0-60mph (0-97km/h): 12.5sec

Northamptonshire circuit dropped the Capris down the grid. In the first heat Gardner used his 7.0-liter V8 to outdrag Ertl's Alpina CSL but a lack of enough suitable tires delayed the Camaro later in the race. Stuck's BMW broke its gearbox and Glemser's Capri was eliminated in an accident, leaving Ertl to win from the Capris of Mass and Fitzpatrick, all of them wowing the Silverstone crowds by cornering regularly on two wheels.

More tire problems sidelined the big Camaro in the second heat, leaving the rapid Mass, Fitzpatrick, Quester, and Bell (in the Ertl Alpina car) to dispute the lead. Quester headed the pack until he ran out of fuel just a few miles from the end of the race, which was eventually taken by Bell's CSL. On aggregate Bell and Ertl won, ahead of Jochen Mass in the RS2600 Capri. BMW took the European Touring Car Championship away from Ford, and CSL driver Toine Hezemans emerged as the drivers' champion. The 'Unbeatable BMW' stickers in the rear windows of many thousands of roadgoing 2002s had been proved right.

The Ford challenge

Ford was already developing its Capris to meet the BMW challenge. The RS2600 homologation special had been replaced by the RS3100, with a 3.1-liter Essex V6 engine and a duck-tail rear spoiler. The racing machines took advantage of these changes to incorporate much bigger aerodynamic aids, and that single-cam, pushrod overhead-valve V6 with 150bhp or so had been developed by Cosworth into a 24-valve, four-cam screamer with more than 400bhp from its 3.5-liters. BMW, too, was going the multi-valve route, with a six-pot version of the cylinder head that had proved so successful on the four-cylinder F2 engines, taking the 3.5-liter race engine to more than 430bhp. But the titanic battle that was promised between the Fords and BMWs never really emerged.

Europe was in the throes of an oil crisis, a consequence of the 1973 Yom Kippur war in the Middle East. Gas prices soared, and in Britain it didn't help that Value Added Tax was applied to gasoline from March 1974, the combined effect of which was to raise the price of a

gallon (4.5 liters) of fuel from 37p in mid-1973 to nearly 60p less than a year later. Suddenly motor sport looked like an expensive and socially irresponsible luxury, and racing programs around Europe were curtailed. The CSLs, in their new midnight blue livery, faced the works Fords just twice in 1974, winning one race and losing the other. But thirsty road cars were suddenly difficult to sell, so while the CSL had proved to be a big success on track, its roadgoing cousin struggled to make a similar impact on the sales charts despite the press raving about the car's speed and particularly about its radical aerodynamic aids, which quickly earned the be-winged CSL the nickname 'Batmobile.' In Germany those wings and spoilers were banned by the government, and German-market CSLs had them packed carefully in the trunk rather than fitted to the car. Though BMW drivers were, perhaps, better able to afford rising fuel prices than most, some of them wanted to be seen to be driving a fuel-efficient, 'responsible' car. BMW responded to the fuel crisis by adding a fuel-efficient 1.8-liter engine to the 5-series range, in the 90bhp 518, alongside the original 2.0-liter 520 and the six-cylinder 525 which had arrived in 1973.

Above: The 7-series of 1977 gave BMW a serious rival to the big Mercedes sedans.

Opposite: The E9 coupés served BMW well, but in 1976 they were replaced by the new 6-series.

That fuel crisis also threatened another rapid BMW road car, the 2002 Turbo. The Turbo's engine technology was derived from that of the turbocharged 2002s which had been built for the 1969 racing season, and in roadgoing production trim the 2.0-liter, KKK-boosted engine produced 170bhp – as much as the 2.8-liter engine in the big E3 sedan, though without the linear delivery of that silken straight-six. In fact the Turbo had a pronounced step in its

Above: Alex Elliot at the 2004 Goodwood Festival of Speed in the Group 5 CSL built for the 1976 season.

Top right: Some CSLs had stripped-out interiors for lightness, but CSLs supplied in the UK usually had full equipment.

Center right: The 'Batmobile' rear wing was illegal in Germany – so on German-market CSLs it was packed in the trunk as a kit of parts for the owner to assemble!

Below right: Originally the CSL's six-cylinder engine was quoted as 3003cc, allowing the race cars to use 3.3-liter engines.

BMW 3.0CSL Turbo (ETCC)

Racing season	1976
Engine	In-line six-cylinder, twin overhead camshafts, 24 valves, aluminum alloy cylinder head
Bore x stroke	92mm x 80mm
Capacity	3191cc
Power	800bhp at 9000rpm
Torque	Not quoted
Fuel system	Kugelfischer mechanical fuel injection
Gearbox	Getrag five-speed manual
Chassis/body	Unitary steel chassis/body with aluminum alloy outer panels, glassfiber wheel arch extensions and aerodynamic package
Suspension	Front: MacPherson struts Rear: semi-trailing arms and coil springs
Brakes	Hydraulically operated, discs all round, four-piston front calipers
Performance	Top speed: approximately 190mph (308km/h)* 0-60mph (0-97km/h): 3.5sec*

* depending on gearing

power curve as the turbocharger came on song, and that vicious delivery caught out many a driver ill-advised enough to open the throttle with some enthusiasm in mid-corner.

Suspension and brakes were naturally uprated to reflect the Turbo's much greater performance, and with its deep front air dam and tacked-on wheel arch extensions covering wide wheels and fat tires the 2002 Turbo clearly meant business. The package was completed by garish BMW Motorsport stripes and a reversed 'turbo' decal designed to catch the attention of the driver ahead when he glanced in his rear view mirror. Europe was in the midst of an oil shortage, but it was this aggressive styling as much as the car's performance – it could deliver a 0-60mph (0-97km/h) time of seven seconds on the way to a top speed in excess of 210km/h (130mph) – which fueled criticism, particularly in Germany. By the end of 1974 and with just 1672 examples built, the 2002 Turbo's production run was over.

Above: Roadgoing CSLs are rare and still highly-prized. This immaculate example dates from 1974.

The Turbo was intended to be the last gasp of the '02 range of cars, drumming up some interest in the aging two-door cars before their replacement, starting in 1975, by the E21 3-series. Despite its massive performance the 2002 Turbo was never intended to be a competition car, though Schnitzer did run a turbocharged version of its 16-valve car. Similar technology would appear on the race tracks a couple of years later, in the 3-series – and before that, BMW would field a turbocharged version of its old warhorse, the CSL.

BMW left the European series to privateers (Alain Peltier's Alpina CSL proved the class of the field) and turned to the IMSA (International Motor Sports Association) series in America, pleasing the crowds and turning in some creditable performances, including a win in the Sebring 12-hours and three more victories for Stuck at Laguna Seca, Riverside, and Talladega. But Porsche's turbocharged sports cars were always going to be favorites against

Jochen Neerpasch: Switching Sides

JOCHEN NEERPASCH began racing in German sedan car events using a Borgward in 1960. After sharing a Shelby Cobra with Chris Amon at Le Mans in 1964 he drove for Porsche in sports car racing and Ford in sedan cars, while at the same time trying to break into Formula 3. Good results were tempered with some big crashes in the unstable Porsche 907s.

In 1968 his career took a different turn when accepted the job of Competitions Manager at the new Ford race and rally operation in Cologne. Neerpasch hired Martin Braungart from Mercedes-Benz to be Chief Engineer of the department, which began by developing the Lotus-engined Escort Twin

Cam for racing and the Capri 2300GT for rallying. Neerpasch then masterminded the appearance of V6 Capris in the European Touring Car Championship, the Cologne cars winning all but one event in 1971. The run continued with a win in the first round of 1972 at Monza, following which Neerpasch and Braungart announced a surprise move to Ford's new main competitor, BMW.

In Munich the pair set up BMW's new Motorsport arm, turned the CSL coupés into race winners, and then backed the M1 project. But Neerpasch moved on again in November 1979, just as BMW's directors were considering whether or not to move into Formula 1 with their turbocharged engine.

Neerpasch nearly pulled off a deal to take the turbo engine with him to Talbot – a move which, had it succeeded, would have changed the face of F1 history.

More recently Neerpasch masterminded the Mercedes-Benz sports car efforts which netted World Championship victories in 1989 and 1990, at the same time setting up another 'Junior Team' which propelled Karl Wendlinger, Heinz-Harald Frentzen, and, most notably, Michael Schumacher into Formula 1.

Below: All three drivers from the BMW Junior Team – Manfred Winkelhock, Marc Surer, and Eddie Cheever – went on to Formula 1. In 1977 they campaigned these BMW 320s.

Above: Jochen Neerpasch (seated left) and his team in 1973. Sitting next to him on the CSL hood is Jean Todt.

the heavier and less powerful BMW touring cars, and the Stuttgart machines succeeded in retaining the championship. For 1976 BMW continued with its IMSA program and ran CSLs in the Group 5 World Championship for Makes, even fielding a monstrous turbocharged CSL for F1's 'SuperSwede' Ronnie Peterson at Silverstone and Dijon. With the bulkhead glowing from the colossal heat output from the 800bhp engine, a hefty appetite for tires (Peterson stopped for new rubber after just 40 miles/64km at Silverstone) and an overwhelmed transmission, the turbo CSL was never going to be a race winner – but it was certainly spectacular. Peterson reported that the turbo car, capable of nigh-on 180mph (290km/h) at Silverstone, would happily spin its overworked rear wheels in third gear...

Meanwhile the Belgian CSL team of Luigi Cimarosti won the 1976 European title for Group 2 cars, now racing to much more restrictive regulations. That was the last year of

Left: The 7-series applied BMW's traditional engineering – including the 'big six' engines and semi-trailing arm rear suspension – to a larger car.

BMW 320 Turbo (ETCC)

Racing seasons	1977-79
Engine	In-line four-cylinder, twin overhead camshaft, 16 valves, aluminum alloy cylinder head
Bore x stroke	89.2mm x 80mm
Capacity	1995cc
Power	500bhp at 9000rpm
Torque	Not quoted
Fuel system	Kugelfischer fuel injection
Gearbox	Five-speed Getrag manual
Chassis/body	Unitary steel chassis/body with aluminum alloy and glassfiber outer panels
Suspension	Front: MacPherson struts Rear: semi-trailing arms and coil springs
Brakes	Hydraulically operated, discs all round
Performance	Top speed: approximately 186mph (300km/h) 0-60mph (0-97km/h): approximately 3.5sec

factory support for the CSL racers, because the CS-series had been replaced by the new 6-series coupé in 1976, but even then privateers carried on racing the CSL. Alpina built up a brand new car from parts, the famous bright green Gösser beer CSL which Dieter Quester used to wrest the European title away from the Luigi team, now running in the red and white striped UFO Jeans livery. Even in 1978 there was no opposition to beat the CSLs, the championship that year falling to Umberto Grano in a Luigi car.

Munich instead turned its attention to the 3-series, which had been criticized in some quarters for its lack of performance and its soft character compared to the classic 2002. A new family of small in-line sixes solved the performance problem, the 140bhp 323i having all the acceleration of the 2002tii but with considerably more comfort and much greater refinement. Even so, the 3-series needed an image boost, and that came in the form of a Group 5 racing version of the 320i to be campaigned in Europe and America. The car was to be powered by the 2.0-liter, 16-valve BMW engine which had been consistently successful in European Formula 2: Jarier's win in the second year of the 2.0-liter formula in 1973 had been followed by wins for Patrick Depailler and Jacques Laffite in BMW-powered cars.

McLaren North America ran a single 320 for Briton David Hobbs in IMSA races, while for Europe Neerpasch recuited three young guns for a 'BMW Junior Team': efforts to provide opportunities for young drivers would become a recurring theme in Neerpasch's motorsport management career. Eddie Cheever, Manfred Winkelhock, and Marc Surer were the three hopefuls, and in testing some of BMW's established drivers also took a turn behind the wheel, Ronnie Peterson demonstrating the 2.0-liter car's exceptional balance by lapping the Paul Ricard circuit in France quicker than he had in a CSL. When the cars raced they provided a marvellous spectacle, all three of the 'Junior Team' drivers battling each other and the competition to be first home. Sometimes the action was a little too close, and emotions ran a little too high. Surer got his race license confiscated for three months after tangling

Above: The 6-series gradually developed more muscle. This is the 3.5-liter 635CSi, introduced in 1978.

BMW 728 E23

Production	1977-79
	(other E23 models 1977-85)
Engine	In-line six-cylinder, single
	overhead camshaft,
	12 valves, aluminum alloy
	cylinder head
Bore x stroke	86mm x 80mm
Capacity	2788cc
Power	170bhp at 6000rpm
Torque	173lbft at 3700rpm
Fuel system	Solex carburetor
Gearbox	Four-speed manual, single
	dry-plate clutch
Chassis/body	Unitary steel chassis/body
Suspension	Front: MacPherson struts
	Rear: semi-trailing arms
	and coil springs
Brakes	Hydraulically operated,
	discs all round
Performance	Top speed: approximately
	120mph (193km/h)
	0-60mph (0-97km/h):
	10.0sec

with Hans Heyer's Escort, and eventually Neerpasch tired of the mechanical carnage, dropping all three Junior Team drivers for one race and replacing them with a better-behaved 'BMW Gentlemen Team' which included Ronnie Peterson and Hans Stuck.

A turbocharged racing version of the 320 quickly followed, David Hobbs using it to win four IMSA rounds in 1977. In Europe the turbo raced sporadically, while the Junior Team wowed crowds with their antics in the normally-aspirated 320s and Schnitzer remained faithful to their 1.4-liter, turbocharged 2002 even though the model had been out of production for quite a while.

Above right: The 323i answered criticisms that the 3-series lacked the sporting appeal of the old 2002.

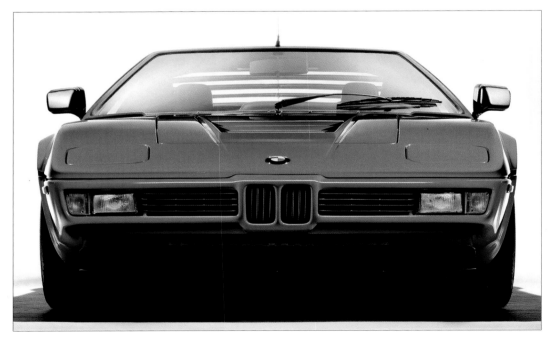

Right: The M1 supercar was a fine machine, but its production was fraught with problems.

Above: Five generations of 5-series BMW. The 5-series has been the mainstay of BMW's range since 1972.

Turbocharging was becoming more and more common on the road by the late 1970s, with BMW's lead having been followed by Porsche, Saab, and subsequently many others. BMW chose not to follow up the 2002 Turbo with a turbocharged roadgoing 3-series, but did turn to turbocharging to provide effortlessly superior power for the top model in a new range of luxury cars.

Bigger and better

The big E3 sedans, which had arrived in 1968 in 2.5-liter form, had developed by way of the 3.0Si and 3.3Li, the latter a long-wheelbase version with extra space for the rear passengers. Their long run ended in 1977, when BMW introduced the final model in the comprehensive overhaul of its range: the 3-series of 1975, 5-series of 1972, and 6-series of 1976 were now joined by the new 7-series. The big new sedan mirrored the styling of the smaller cars, with BMW's characteristic four-headlamp front end complete with 'kidney' grille, and clean lines with a generous glass area. The engine range was mostly familiar, too, with carburetored 728 and 730 models and a fuel-injected 733i. A revised, fuel-injected range introduced in 1979 included 728i, 732i, and 735i models. For some markets there was also a 745i with 3.2-liter version of the familiar 'big six' boosted by a single KKK turbocharger to deliver 252bhp. The '745' designation reflected the racing practice of classifying turbocharged cars by multiplying their engine capacity by 1.4, implying that the 3.2-liter turbo engine was the equivalent of a 4.5-liter normally-aspirated unit. Certainly the 745i performed as though it had plenty of cubic inches under the hood, accelerating from rest to 62mph (100km/h) in less than eight seconds and going on to an impressive top speed in the region of 140mph (225km/h).

Turbocharging would also be central to BMW's new motorsport plans. In addition to the M1 project (see box on page 100), BMW was aiming to enter Formula 1 as an engine supplier. The engine was to be based on the 2.0-liter turbo unit that had seen service in the 320 turbo touring cars, itself a descendant of the production four-cylinder motor which had made its debut all those years ago in the 1500 Neue Klasse sedan. Alex von Falkenhausen had deliberately designed it to be a strong engine, but in the next few years it would become clear to everyone just how amazingly capable that little engine could be.

BMW 323i E21

Production	1977-83
Engine	In-line six-cylinder, single overhead camshaft, 12 valves, aluminum alloy cylinder head
Bore x stroke	80mm x 76.8mm
Capacity	2316cc
Power	143bhp at 6000rpm
Torque	140lbft at 4500rpm
Fuel system	Bosch K-Jetronic fuel injection
Gearbox	Four-speed manual, single dry-plate clutch
Chassis/body	Unitary steel chassis/body
Suspension	Front: MacPherson struts Rear: semi-trailing arms and coil springs
Brakes	Hydraulically operated, discs all round
Performance	Top speed: approximately 124mph (200km/h) 0-60mph (0-97km/h): 8.8sec

'Procar' and M1 – a BMW supercar

DWINDLING INTEREST in sports car racing during the 1970s prompted calls for a more 'relevant' formula with a closer link to production cars. The Group 5 'Silhouette Formula' proposed that cars could be extensively modified, provided that they looked the same as the production machines from the side, and provided that major items such as the engine were broadly similar in type and location to the original machine.

BMW backed the Group 5 proposals, and Jochen Neerpasch set about creating a low-volume BMW supercar on which to base its racer. This was to become the M1. The BMW Turbo concept car of 1972 provided the basic shape, which was refined by ItalDesign, while the CSL racing developments provided a ready-made engine. In 1976 the famous Italian supercar maker Lamborghini was engaged to turn the basic idea into a workable road car and then build the 400 units required for homologation.

But Lamborghini was in desperate financial trouble, and the cash-starved development process dragged on and on. The 1977 racing season came and went. By the spring of the following year BMW had had enough, and engaged German coachbuilder Baur to build the cars instead.

Group 5 had never really emerged as the front-running sports car category, so to maximize the exposure it got from the M1,

BMW created a new racing series, Procar, supporting eight rounds of the F1 World Championship. At first the idea was that the top five on the grid for each Grand Prix would also appear in the Procar race, but that plan was swamped by a welter of contractual difficulties. But some Grand Prix stars did appear, battling it out alongside more than a dozen privateer M1s in the richest and fastest one-make series yet devised. Procar ran for just two seasons, Niki Lauda emerging as 1979 champion and Nelson Piquet winning in 1980.

Above: Procar drivers, from left: Jacques Laffite, Didier Pironi, Alan Jones, Nelson Piquet (the 1980 Procar champion), and Carlos Reutemann.

Below left: Brabham F1 driver Nelson Piquet would go on to win the F1 World Championship powered by BMW engines.

Below: The Procar M1s supported eight Grands Prix – here they round the Mirabeau corner at Monaco.

BMW M1

Production	1979-80
Engine	In-line six-cylinder, single overhead camshaft, 24 valves, aluminum alloy cylinder head
Bore x stroke	93.4mm x 84mm
Capacity	3453cc
Power	277bhp at 6500rpm
Torque	239lbft at 5000rpm
Fuel system	Kugelfischer-Bosch mechanical fuel injection
Gearbox	Five-speed manual, twin-plate clutch
Chassis/body	Steel tubular chassis with glassfiber body
Suspension	Wishbones and coil springs all round
Brakes	Hydraulically operated, discs all round
Performance	Top speed: approximately 161mph (259km/h) 0-60mph (0-97km/h): 5.6sec

Above: Jean-Pierre Jarier, former BMW-powered F2 champion, was another Procar driver.

Right: Niki Lauda's Project 4 Racing M1 won the Procar series in 1979.

Below: The M1 was the first BMW road car from the company's Motorsport arm.

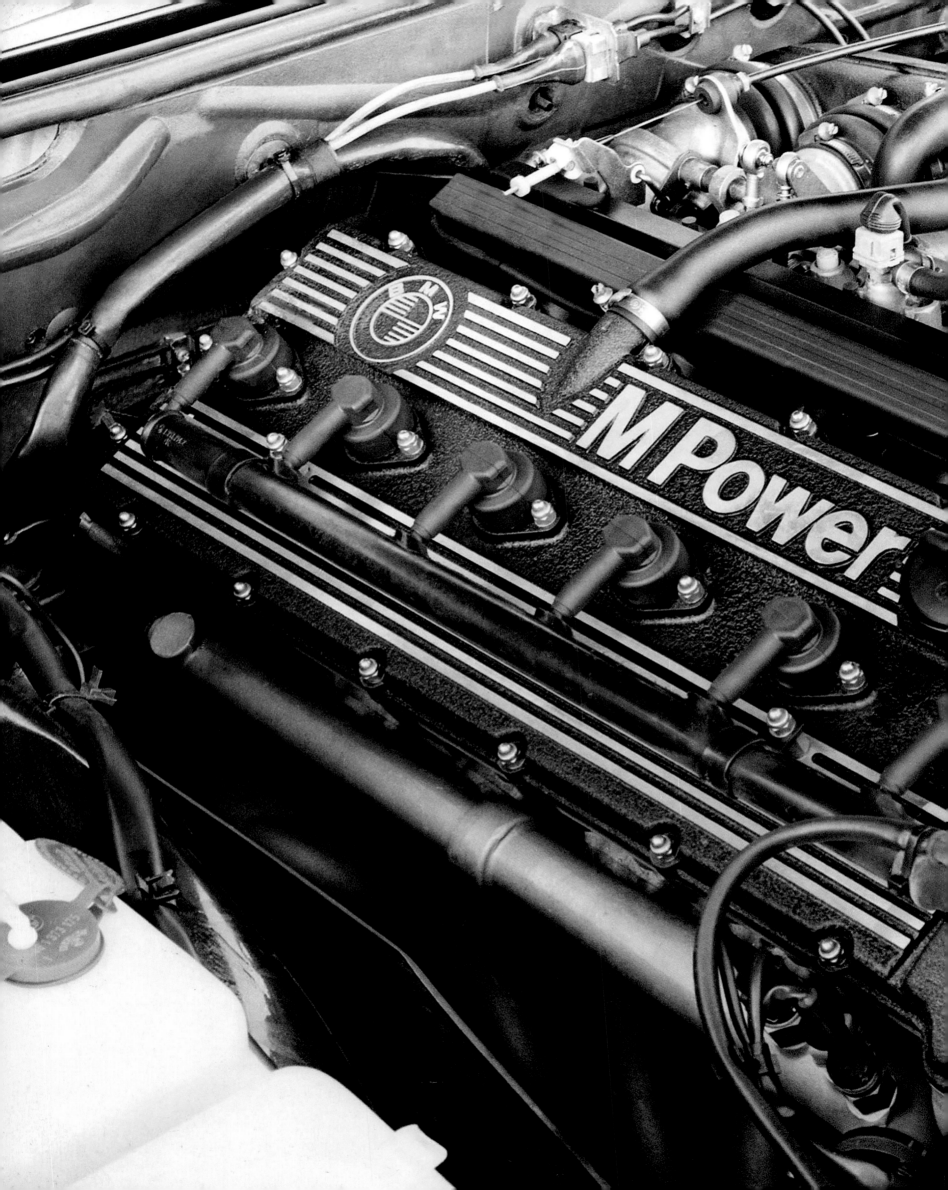

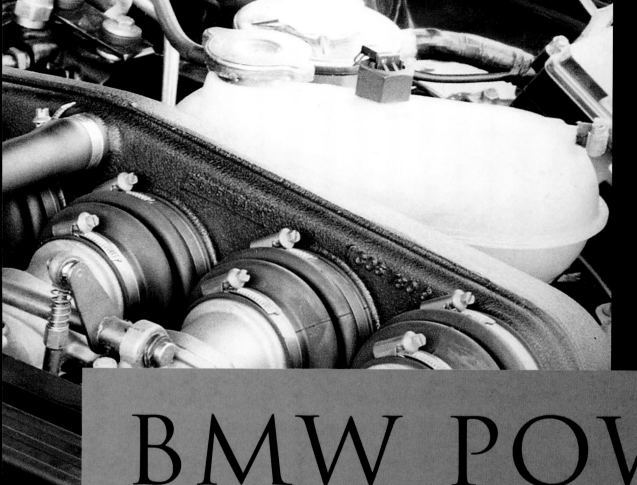

BMW POWER
1980-85

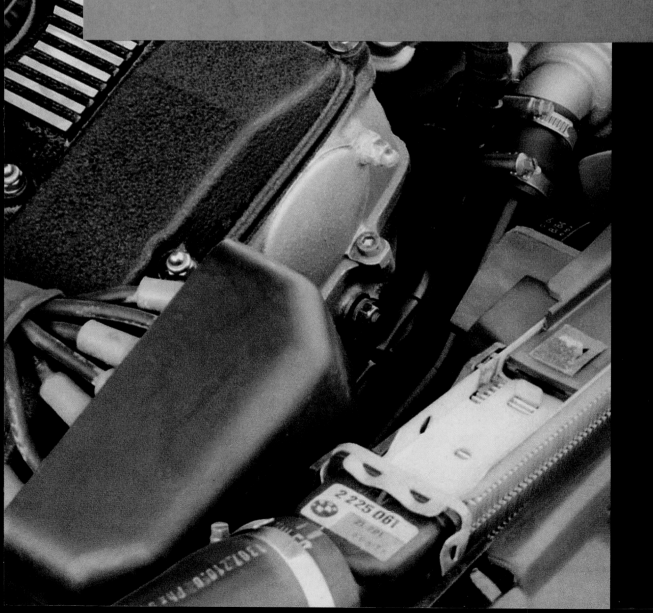

Previous pages: The Motorsport straight-six engine was derived directly from experience with the racing CSLs and the M1. It would power a generation of extraordinary road cars.

BMW M535i E12

Production	1980-81
Engine	In-line six-cylinder, single overhead camshaft, 12 valves, aluminum alloy cylinder head
Bore x stroke	93.4mm x 84mm
Capacity	3453cc
Power	218bhp at 5200rpm
Torque	228lbft at 4000rpm
Fuel system	Bosch L-Jetronic fuel injection
Gearbox	Five-speed Getrag manual, single dry-plate clutch
Chassis/body	Unitary steel chassis/body with aluminum alloy outer panels
Suspension	Front: MacPherson struts Rear: semi-trailing arms and coil springs
Brakes	Hydraulically operated, discs all round
Performance	Top speed: approximately 140mph (225km/h) 0-60mph (0-97km/h): 7.0sec

Above right: The second-generation 5-series debuted in 1981, looking much the same as before. This is the six-cylinder 525i.

Right: The E12 M535i driver was held firmly in place by a cord-trimmed Recaro seat and grasped an M1-style leather steering wheel.

WHILE THE 5-series had not enjoyed the same kind of racing career as the CSL coupé, it had been seen in production sedan racing in Europe, following on from some successful seasons' racing with the big 3.0Si sedans in the early 1970s. The 5-series had been most successful in South Africa, where a curious set of regulations allowed 'production' sedans to sport modifications similar to those seen in the Group 2 'modified sedans' category in Europe – spoilers, wide wheels and add-on wheel arches, and much-modified engines were all allowed. Some of those modifications found their way onto special one-off road cars built for lucky customers of BMW Motorsport, and in South Africa a package of performance parts appeared on a limited-production road car known as the 530i Motorsport Limited Edition, for which BMW Motorsport in Munich had been responsible. Europe had to wait for a high-performance version of the 5-series, but the car that would finally emerge would not only be worth the wait, it would launch a whole new genre of BMW road cars.

The existing 5-series range was topped by a 2.8-liter 528i in Europe and a 3.0 liter 530i in America, both using the 'big six' engine. The 3.5-liter version of that engine originally developed for the CSL racing program (despite initial misgivings about the lack of cooling passages between the bores) had already been slotted into the 6-series and 7-series. In this production form the bore was fractionally smaller at 93.4mm, which combined with an 84mm stroke to displace 3453cc. With a 9.3:1 compression ratio, the Bosch L-Jetronic fuel injected engine developed 218bhp and 228lbft, and it slotted into the 5-series shell to produce a car called the M535i. The big six was mated to a Getrag five-speed gearbox with a 'dog-leg' first gear, which brought the most-used four gears into the familiar 'H' pattern and relegated first gear to a left-and-back position. That meant the first to second gear change was a little slow as the driver had to negotiate the dog-leg, but even so *Autocar* recorded a scorching 0-60mph (0-97km/h) sprint time of 7.1 seconds for the M535i, more than a second and a half ahead of its nearest rival (and quicker than the heavier 635CSi and 735i which shared the same engine). The chassis was uprated to cope using stiffer springs, fatter anti-roll bars and Bilstein dampers, together with bigger 635CSi brakes. Externally there was a deep body-colored air dam under the front bumper and a flexible, black spoiler on the trunk lid, plus 6.5x14in Mahle alloy wheels. High back Recaro seats dominated the interior, and the driver was treated to a three-spoke M1 steering wheel.

Below: The E12 M535i was amazingly rapid for a big sedan. It marked the first application of the 'M' badge to a BMW sedan.

BMW 525e E28

Production	1983-87
Engine	In-line six-cylinder, single overhead camshaft, 12 valves, aluminum alloy cylinder head
Bore x stroke	84mm x 81mm
Capacity	2693cc
Power	125bhp at 4250rpm
Torque	177lbft at 3250rpm
Fuel system	Bosch Motronic engine management
Gearbox	Five-speed manual, single dry-plate clutch or four-speed ZF automatic
Chassis/body	Unitary steel chassis/body
Suspension	Front: MacPherson struts Rear: semi-trailing arms and coil springs
Brakes	Hydraulically operated, discs all round
Performance	Top speed: approximately 112mph (180km/h) 0-60mph (0-97km/h):10.5secs

Right: The E28 5-series looked very similar to the previous E12, but was lighter and more aerodynamic in its styling.

Above: The 2.8-liter six-cylinder engine was a popular option, giving the 528i speed and refinement.

Despite the M535i's considerable appeal as a high-performance, luxury sedan, its production run was curtailed by the introduction in 1981 of a new E28 5-series sedan. At first glance the new cars looked much the same as the old, and the E28 body shared door and roof panels with the old car, but there were numerous detail improvements. Careful analysis of the structure resulted in a car which was a little lighter than its predecessor, but at the same time offered better crash performance, while clever work on the body shape resulted in a lower coefficient of drag and less lift at high speed. Unusually for a BMW, the hood opened conventionally rather than hinging forward.

A new generation

Though the new 5-series shared its suspension layout with the old car, there were again changes in detail. At the front, the lower ends of the MacPherson struts were now formed by two separate links instead of a single wishbone, an idea first seen on the 7-series. Careful design of the geometry resulted in an increase in steering offset as the wheels were steered away from center, giving better steering feel without excessive kickback near the straight-ahead position.

Also new was a Service Interval Indicator, a sequence of green, yellow, and red lights which indicted when the 5-series needed servicing. The computer-controlled indicator calculated service requirements based on the mileage the car traveled while also taking into account the number of cold starts and the amount of time the engine spent at high revs. A trip computer – already available on the 7-series – offering information on fuel consumption, range, average speed, and estimated arrival time was an option on the new car.

1500 nearly two decades before. Rosche's men quickly found that the best blocks for the turbo engine were not brand new, but a couple of years old and well-used – the aging process seemed to remove the inherent stresses in the block casting and make for a more reliable engine.

By the middle of the 1981 season the team was ready to practice the car in public, again at Silverstone, where it posted the third-fastest time. But Brabham stuck with its Cosworth-powered car for the race and for the rest of the season, which ended with Piquet as World Champion, just a point ahead of Williams driver Carlos Reutemann.

The BMW-engined Brabham made its Grand Prix debut at the first round of the 1982 championship, in South Africa, where Piquet crashed the BT50 after just three laps and team mate Riccardo Patrese's car suffered a turbo failure. The team reverted to the Cosworth-powered cars for Brazil and Long Beach, but Piquet tried the BMW-engined car again at Zolder for the Belgian Grand Prix. Ferrari withdrew from the race after Gilles Villeneuve was killed in a practice crash, and John Watson's McLaren won a somber victory while Piquet brought home the Brabham-BMW in fifth place.

Mixed results

At Monaco two weeks later, Piquet again ran the BMW-engined Brabham while Patrese drove the Cosworth-powered car. Despite putting his Brabham off the road for the second race in succession, Patrese contrived to rejoin and win the event, inheriting the lead after the Renaults of René Arnoux and Alain Prost both crashed out, Didier Pironi's Ferrari expired in the tunnel with an electrical fault, and Andrea de Cesaris' Alfa ran out of fuel. Piquet, too, was a retiree, the Brabham's innovative transverse gearbox in pieces after 49 tough laps of Monte Carlo.

A dismal race followed in Detroit: Piquet failed to qualify, while Patrese retired the Cosworth-powered Brabham after an accident six laps into the race. But a week later in Montreal for the Canadian Grand Prix, it was a very different story. The race got off to a tragic start when Pironi stalled on the front of the grid and Ricardo Paletti was killed when his Osella rammed the stationary Ferrari. The race was restarted, and Piquet lifted Munich spirits by taking the victory, with team mate Patrese second in the Cosworth car. At round nine of the championship, the Dutch Grand Prix, the Brabham-BMW again went well, finishing second to Pironi's hard-charging Ferrari.

Both drivers had BMW power for the British Grand Prix at Silverstone, Patrese setting the second fastest time in practice with Piquet in third – but the big news was Brabham practicing a tire and fuel pit stop, then unheard of in F1. The Brabhams started the race half-full of fuel and running on soft tires, the intention being to stop during the race for fuel and fresh rubber. But Patrese was eliminated in an accident right at the start and Piquet's car

Above: Brazilian Nelson Piquet won the F1 World Championship twice with Brabham, giving BMW its first crown in 1983.

Above: The 1983 Brabham team, reunited at the Goodwood Festival of Speed 20 years on from their championship success. Nelson Piquet is in the middle with the green jacket, mustachioed Gordon Murray is at the back.

Opposite: The Brabham reintroduced fuel and tire stops to Formula 1 in 1982.

Right: Gordon Murray's Brabham BT53 chassis exploited awesome BMW turbo power in 1983.

Brabham-BMW BT52

Racing season	1983
Engine	In-line four-cylinder, twin overhead camshafts, 16 valves, aluminum alloy cylinder head
Bore x stroke	89.2mm x 60mm
Capacity	1499cc
Power	Approximately 600bhp at 9500rpm (over 1000bhp in qualifying tune)
Torque	325lbft at 8500rpm
Fuel system	Bosch/Kugelfischer mechanical fuel injection, single KKK turbocharger and intercooler
Gearbox	Five-speed manual, single dry-plate clutch
Chassis/body	Carbon fiber monocoque
Suspension	Double wishbones and coil springs (inboard at front)
Brakes	Ventilated steel discs, later Hitco carbon discs/pads
Performance	Top speed: approximately 200mph (322km/h) 0-60mph (0-97km/h): less than 4.0sec

dropped out with fuel injection problems, so neither car reached its scheduled pit stop. More reliability problems dogged the team in the French Grand Prix, where both Brabham-BMWs expired with dead engines leaving the Renaults to dominate the race.

At the German Grand Prix Patrese's engine suffered a piston failure and Piquet crashed, Patrick Tambay winning the race in the sole remaining Ferrari (Pironi had crashed badly in practice) to become the seventh different winner of the season. It was much the same story in Austria the following weekend, where Patrese's BMW engine failed after 27 laps while the Italian was leading the race and Piquet's engine called time just a few minutes later – but the cars did at least last long enough for Brabham to perform its first mid-race pit stop. This time Elio de Angelis took the checkered flag, his Lotus just a few feet ahead of a hard charging Keke Rosberg's Williams.

Rosberg got his own back in the Swiss Grand Prix at the French Dijon-Prenois track, where Piquet and Patrese brought the Brabham-BMWs home in fourth and fifth. At Monza turbo cars ruled, René Arnoux's Renault taking the flag ahead of Tambay and Mario Andretti in the Ferraris. But the Brabham-BMWs failed to finish, both experiencing clutch failures. And the team ended the year in a downbeat fashion: Patrese had another clutch failure at the final race of the season, the Caesars Palace Grand Prix in Las Vegas, and Piquet's engine destroyed a spark plug. After a scrappy F1 season in which 11 different drivers won races, Rosberg emerged as champion with Patrese 10th and Piquet 11th. Brabham were ninth in the constructors' championship, which was won by Ferrari. Elsewhere in the world of motorsport, Corrado Fabi notched up BMW's sixth European Formula 2 Championship victory at the end of a thrilling season, and the signs were that F1 glory would not be far behind, if reliability could be developed into the Brabham-BMWs.

At Brabham Gordon Murray planned an evolution of the BMW-powered BT50 for the new season, at the same time incorporating changes demanded by new regulations. In

Below: Rule changes meant that the BT53 ran without the long 'ground effects' side-pods of previous F1 cars.

previous years F1 cars had used the air flow under the car to create 'ground effect,' which sucked the car down on to the road, increasing grip. Venturi-shaped tunnels under the car were an essential part of the system, along with sliding skirts on the side-pods to seal in the under-car vacuum they created. The 1983 'flat bottom' rules banned the venturi tunnels and the skirts in an effort to curb rising cornering speeds.

Below: Piquet leads the Renault of Alain Prost at Zandvoort in 1983. The pair would crash out later in the race.

Piquet used the new Brabham BT52 to good effect straight out of the box. At the Brazilian Grand Prix in March he qualified fourth and then won the race ahead of pole man and reigning champion Keke Rosberg in the Cosworth-engined Williams, the first time Brabham had won using its new planned-pitstop strategy. Rosberg also refueled mid-race, suffering a fire in the process, and was later disqualified for a push-start. Patrese's Brabham retired, but another BMW-powered car did finish: Gunther Schmid's ATS team had begun to use Munich's engines, and an ATS-BMW D6 was the last car running at the end of

Below: After 630 days in F1, BMW claimed its first title. Piquet crosses the line to take third place in the 1983 South African Grand Prix, and win the World Championship, in the Brabham-BMW BT52.

the race. The driver was Manfred Winkelhock, who five years earlier had been part of Neerpasch's BMW Junior Team.

At Long Beach Winkelhock's ATS crashed out on lap 4, Piquet's throttle jammed on lap 52 and Patrese's distributor failed right at the end of the race, though he was classified 10th. John Watson and Niki Lauda proved there was still life in the Cosworth V8 by coming

Brabham: Turbo Champions

JACK BRABHAM was the first man to win a Grand Prix in a car bearing his own name, at the French Grand Prix in 1966. 'Black Jack' won the drivers' championship that year, and the Brabham team took the constructor's cup, repeating the win the following year when New Zealander Denny Hulme was the champion driver.

Brabham's partner Ron Tauranac assumed control of the team in 1970, and sold it during the following year to Bernie Ecclestone. South African Gordon Murray took over as the team's design chief, and instituted a new line of neat Cosworth DFV-powered cars with a triangular body section,

carrying fuel low in the monocoque to improve the car's center of gravity.

In 1976 Brabham switched to the bulky Alfa Romeo flat-12 engine, but its wide, low shape prevented Brabham following the ground effects' route pioneered by Lotus. Instead Murray concocted the BT46B 'fan car,' with an engine-mounted fan sucking air from under the car. Lauda won the Swedish

Grand Prix in 1978, but subsequently the car was banned as unsafe.

Brabham returned to the DFV V8 engine, then switched to BMW turbos during 1982. After Murray and Piquet had departed, the team spent a year out of F1, then returned for 1989 with the Sergio Rinland-designed BT58. But success eluded the team, and it folded at the end of 1992.

through from 22nd and 23rd on the grid to record a 1-2 for McLaren. Turbo engines were back at the top in France, where Prost's Renault won with Piquet second, Patrese and Winkelhock both retiring with engine trouble. At Imola, Piquet's BMW engine failed and Patrese crashed, but Winkelhock's ATS made it to the finish in 11th place.

Through the middle of the season Piquet scored points in most races. The Brazilian finished second in Monaco, fourth at Spa and fourth again in Detroit, where Brabham fooled everyone by not stopping mid-race. Piquet retired with a failed throttle linkage in Canada, but was back on the podium at Silverstone, finishing second behind Alain Prost's Renault while Patrese and Winkelhock both went out with engine problems. It was Piquet's turn to experience problems in Germany, with a fuel leak leading to an engine fire, but Patrese had a good day and finished third behind Arnoux's Ferrari and de Cesaris' turbo Alfa.

Piquet finished third in Austria, and then qualified on pole position at the Dutch Grand Prix but could not take advantage, tangling with Prost's Renault to the detriment of both. At the time Prost was leading the battle for the championship, but not for long: Piquet was back on the top step of the podium at Monza, then won the European Grand Prix at Brands Hatch. By now BMW was using a new fuel developed by German chemical company BASF, which

Above: Piquet in the Brabham BT52 during his second championship-winning season, 1983. At Paul Ricard he split the two Renaults, finishing 30 seconds behind winner Alain Prost.

Above left: The 1.5-liter BMW Turbo was based on a production design.

solved some of the problems experienced earlier in the season with engine damage due to pre-ignition and also liberated considerable extra power from the turbo four.

Prost had finished second at Brands, which meant Piquet was just a point behind going into the final race at Kyalami in South Africa. First blood went to the Brabham-BMWs, with Piquet and Patrese qualifying second and third behind Tambay's Ferrari and Prost's Renault back on the third row of the grid. Piquet led early on, while Prost fought to catch the Brabham-BMWs, but the Renault's turbo failed after 35 laps. Patrese and de Cesaris got ahead of Piquet, who cruised to third place, four points and his second World Championship. Brabham-BMW could do no better than third in the Constructor's Cup, however, behind the more consistent Ferrari and Renault teams.

Efficiency in action

Off the track, however, the emphasis was more about saving fuel than winning performance battles. Fuel prices were on the rise again, and luxury car makers (and buyers) were suddenly cast as the villains, wasting the precious natural resources that others were making efforts to save. Just as it had done ten years earlier when Europe was in the grip of the Yom Kippur War oil crisis, BMW replied with a high-economy version of the 5-series for buyers who wanted BMW quality and luxury without the stigma that increasingly attached to high

Above: Four doors made the compact E30 3-series a viable option for enthusiastic drivers with families.

performance cars. The new car was called the 525e, the e representing the Greek letter 'eta,' the engineering symbol for efficiency. Under the hood of the 525e sat an enlarged version of the 'small six' that powered the 520i, tuned to give the same power output as the 2.0-liter unit (125bhp) but a much higher torque peak of 177lbft. High overall gearing was achieved using a 2.93:1 final drive, which gave the 525e the opportunity to return surprisingly economical fuel consumption figures. Even so, the torquey engine made it a satisfying and swift car to drive.

Even more torque was available from another new engine which went into the 5-series in 1983. BMW had begun development of a diesel engine back in 1975, no doubt spotting the large proportion of mid-size Mercedes sales taken by Stuttgart's five-cylinder oil-burners. Two versions were made available, a sloth-like 86bhp 524d and a turbocharged 524td with a more respectable 115bhp, but these were a long way from the astonishing performance diesels that BMW would introduced nearer the end of the century.

A fuel-injected 518i replaced the carburetored 518 in 1984, but BMW was not neglecting the performance end of the market. The 535i and M535i arrived at the same time, bringing the performance of the previous M535i to the newer E28 range. The 3.5-liter engine differed marginally in its dimensions but was still claimed to produce the same 218bhp, turning the

Left: The long-running 24-valve Motorsport engine Rosche created turned the 6-series into this, the M635CSi – a Porsche 928 rival.

Paul Rosche: Man of Power

BORN IN Munich in 1934, Paul Rosche trained as an engineer at Munich's Polytechnic and joined Alex von Falkenhausen's engine development department in 1957. Rosche worked on the road and race engines BMW used during the 1960s and then became part of the 'BMW Underground Racing Team' that ran unofficial BMW engines in F2 after the works' withdrawal. As BMW became a recognized force in touring car racing, F2 and later F1, Rosche's ready smile and partiality to the odd

stein of weissbeer became familiar features at race tracks around Europe.

In 1975 Rosche became General Manager of BMW Motorsport and continued to lead the company's competition engine development program. Rosche was the instigator of the turbo F1 project and later of the M3 competition engines. He was also the architect of the awesome 627bhp V12 engine which powered the McLaren F1 road car to its world record maximum speed of 240mph (386km/h).

Rosche continued working on BMW engines until his retirement in 1999 – just after he had completed the E41 3.0-liter V10 engine for the new BMW-Williams Grand Prix car. He was succeeded by Dr. Werner Laurenz, formerly of Audi.

Above: Paul Rosche led BMW's engine development operations.

Left: Paul Rosche (left) with Nelson Piquet (in car) and Dr. Mario Theissen (current BMW F1 engine designer) at the Goodwood Festival of Speed in July 2003, with the championship-winning 1983 BT52.

Above: The 24-valve straight-six in the M635CSi was derived from the racing CSL engines.

Left: The M635CSi offered supercar performance with space for four.

BMW M635CSi

Production	1983-89
Engine	In-line six-cylinder, twin overhead camshafts, 24 valves, aluminum alloy cylinder head
Bore x stroke	93.4mm x 84mm
Capacity	3453cc
Power	286bhp at 6500rpm
Torque	251lbft at 4500rpm
Fuel system	Bosch Motronic engine management
Gearbox	Five-speed ZF manual, single dry-plate clutch
Chassis/body	Unitary steel chassis/body
Suspension	Front: MacPherson struts Rear: semi-trailing arms and coil springs
Brakes	Hydraulically operated, discs all round
Performance	Top speed: approximately 158mph (254km/h) 0-60mph (0-97km/h): 6.3sec

EVER MORE COMPETITIVE
1985-94

Previous pages: Bernard Beguin won the 1987 Tour de Corse rally in a Prodrive M3.

Above: Marc Surer returns to the cockpit of the Arrows-BMW A8 at the Goodwood Festival of Speed.

BMW DEVELOPED some impressive roadgoing cars in the late 1970s and early '80s, and the M5 in particular deserved the reputation it won for awesome speed blended with civilized road manners, practicality, and comfort. But the next headline-grabbing motor car from Munich was very different: instead of being an autobahn-burner it was to be a homologation special for racing, a car which existed for no reason other than to provide a good basis for a production sedan racing car.

At least one prototype was built with the 3.5-liter, 24-valve Motorsport engine, as used in the M635CSi and M5, shoehorned under a 3-series hood. But, though powerful, the big six was also heavy and that extra front-end weight disturbed the handling of the compact E30. Instead Paul Rosche's team produced a new 16-valve engine which was effectively a shortened version of the big six, based on the faithful M12 block with a 16-valve head which was essentially two-thirds of the head from the M635CSi. With the same 93.4mm bore and 84mm stroke as the 3.5-liter six, the new four-cylinder engine displaced 2.3 liters and produced 200bhp in its original version. When the German government made it clear that cars equipped with catalytic converters and running on unleaded fuel would be given significant tax advantages, BMW quickly developed a catalyzed version which still generated 195bhp and showed little reduction in torque. Even in this slightly lower-powered form the new Motorsport 3-series, predictably titled M3, was capable of 143mph (230km/h).

But the M3 was more than just a 3-series with a hot new engine. The car's chassis had been comprehensively revised by a team led by Thomas Ammerschläger, who had worked at

BMW M3 E30

Production	1986-90
Engine	In-line four-cylinder, twin overhead camshafts, 16 valves, aluminum alloy cylinder head
Bore x stroke	93.4mm x 84mm
Capacity	2302cc
Power	200bhp at 6750rpm
Torque	177lbft at 4750rpm
Fuel system	Bosch Motronic engine management
Gearbox	Five-speed Getrag manual, single dry-plate clutch
Chassis/body	Unitary steel chassis/body
Suspension	Front: MacPherson struts Rear: semi-trailing arms and coil springs
Brakes	Hydraulically operated, discs all round
Performance	Top speed: 146mph (235km/h) 0-60mph (0-97km/h): 7.1sec

Zakspeed on its racing turbo Capris and at Audi on the four-wheel-drive quattro. Stiffer springs and anti-roll bars, and twin-tube gas dampers, were obvious modifications for this ultimate 3-series, but the changes also stretched to different pick-up points for the front anti-roll bar, more caster to improve steering feel and a quicker steering ratio. Stub axles from the E28 5-series were used because this provided bigger wheel bearings. The transmission was uprated with a ZF limited-slip differential, a heavy-duty clutch, and a tough Getrag gearbox – except in the US, where the M3 used the 325i Sport gearbox because it was thought buyers would object to the Getrag's dog-leg pattern.

The lighter two-door 3-series shell was chosen for the M3, but again there were significant differences between the M3 and lesser models. The deep front air dam and trunk-mounted rear wing were obvious additions, as were the extended wheel arches, but less apparent was the higher line of the trunk lid and the shallower line of the rear window, both of which helped to improve the airflow over the back of the car at racing speeds.

The M3 made its bow at the Frankfurt show in 1985, but production did not get under way until late in 1986, and racing activity had to wait until 1987. In the meantime BMW's turbo engine continued to perform in F1, being seen in a wider range of cars in 1986. Nelson Piquet had moved to Williams-Honda and Riccardo Patrese had returned to Brabham, where he was partnered by the Italian Elio de Angelis, late of Lotus. Gordon Murray's latest chassis, the BT55, was a radical 'low line' design with its four-cylinder BMW turbo engine cranked over at 72 degrees to the vertical to keep the car's center of gravity low, minimize frontal area and maximize clean airflow to the rear wing. But the design was dogged by problems, first with the low-line bevel gear transmission and later by oil scavenge problems caused by the canted-over engine.

Above left: A powerful 16-valve engine and well-sorted handling made the M3 a formidable road car, and an excellent basis for racing machines.

Opposite: The M3 entered – and won – touring car championships all over the world, beginning in 1987.

BMW M3 (World Touring Car Championship)
Racing season 1987

Engine	In-line four-cylinder, twin overhead camshafts, 16 valves, aluminum alloy cylinder head
Bore x stroke	93.4mm x 84mm
Capacity	2302cc
Power	320bhp at 8200rpm
Torque	Not quoted
Fuel system	Bosch Motronic engine management
Gearbox	Five-speed Getrag manual, single dry-plate clutch
Chassis/body	Unitary steel chassis/body
Suspension	Front: MacPherson struts. Rear: semi-trailing arms and coil springs
Brakes	Hydraulically operated, discs all round
Performance	Top speed: approximately 175mph (282km/h) 0-60mph (0-97km/h): approximately 5.0 sec

Arrows ran 'upright' BMW turbo engines in the A8s driven by Marc Surer and Thierry Boutsen. Toleman had been bought out and re-branded as Benetton, and drivers Gerhard Berger and Teo Fabi enjoyed BMW power in their Benetton B186s. In fact the first points of the year for the BMW runners were won by Berger at the first race in Brazil, where the Austrian finished sixth, two laps down on Piquet's winning Williams. Both Benettons finished in the points in Spain, and Berger was third in the San Marino Grand Prix, where Patrese's Brabham was classified sixth despite running out of fuel. There was little good news from the Monaco race, and then the Brabham team suffered an appalling blow: during testing at the Paul Ricard circuit in France, the BT55 driven by the likeable and talented de Angelis

S-class, which was a big car that contrived to look even bigger, was condemned as excessive.

BMW's V12 also went into a replacement for the 6-series coupé, which was increasingly seen as old-fashioned and outdated. Early plans were for a direct replacement, but with the arrival of Wolfgang Reitzle as BMW's new engineering chief, the new car took on a much more ambitious role – that of taking BMW into the rarefied arena of Porsches and top-end Mercedes coupés. It was called the 850i, and was available with the latest electronic gizmos including traction control, electronically-controlled dampers, and AHK, the German abbreviation for an active rear-wheel steering system which automatically corrected the car's attitude in corners. Despite this attention to handling and grip the 850i was more a fast GT than a true sports car. The notably opinionated *Fast Lane* magazine even ran its 850i test as a cover story with the headline 'Is this a sports car? We say no.' But for the purpose for which it was designed, the swift and refined 850i had few peers.

The 850i was just about as different as it could be from another sporting BMW, the Z1, which had started rolling off the production lines in 1988. This machine was the first product from BMW Technik, a new division set up in 1984 to investigate advanced design ideas and to create small-volume niche-market cars. The Z1 incorporated a number of innovations, including an unusual structure with a steel perimeter frame and bonded-in composite floor. There were unstressed plastic external panels, electrically-powered doors which dropped

Below: The second generation M3, based on the E36 3-series of 1990, was a more refined road car than its predecessor.

Above: Regulations for the ADAC GT Cup allowed more extensive modifications to the car than was the case in the British Touring Car Championship. This is Johnny Cecotto in the BMW M3 GTR in 1993.

Right: BMW's British championship opposition came from front-wheel-drive cars in 1993.

down into the sills (you could drive the car with them lowered) and the transversely-mounted exhaust muffler at the back of the car formed an under-car wing to cut lift at speed. Though the Z1's looks (which seem to have influenced the later 8-series) and cart-like handling have earned it near legendary status among BMW enthusiasts (despite its unspectacular performance, due to its considerable weight) the most enduring feature proved to be the rear suspension, another innovation known as the 'Z-axle'. This was one of a number of multi-link rear suspension systems which arrived in the motor industry in the 1980s when computing power became available to calculate accurately the phenomenally complicated behavior of these complex systems.

New generations

The Z1 won many a headline, but other BMW machines being readied for production were far more important in sales and financial terms. The E34 was a new generation of mid-range 5-series sedans, blending styling elements from the E30 3-series and the E32 7-series into a harmonious whole. As ever the mechanical underpinnings of the car built upon the sucessful elements of previous models, there being little reason to make major changes when BMWs were already regarded as some of the best driver's cars on the market – or, as the advertising slogan had it, the 'Ultimate Driving Machines.'

But that did not apply to the E36 3-series which arrived in 1990. The E30 3-series it replaced had been a conservative design, and the new car was much more adventurous in its styling and its engineering. Previous 3-series models had started life as two-door cars, with a four-door E30 added later – and this proved so popular that the E36 was introduced in four-door form, with a two-door (called a Coupé) following on. The E36's styling further developed the 7-series/5-series theme, with a much more rounded, aerodynamic look than the previous generation. The wide stance and faired-in headlamps added to the efficient appearance, and avoided the criticisms that some had levelled at BMW's two larger sedan ranges for being too similar in appearance.

Under the skin the E36 carried over its M40 four-cylinder engines (in the 316i and 318i) from the last of the E30 cars, and its M50 six-cylinder engines (320i, 325i) from the recently-introduced E34 5-series. Of greater note was a very different rear suspension system to any of BMW's previous sedans, a development of the multi-link Z-axle first seen on the Z1 sports car that was also now in use on the 850i.

The pace of development at BMW was at a level never seen before, and the E36 suffered as a result. While there was nothing wrong with the major mechanical components, the interior trim of the new car proved to be less than durable. Dashboards rattled and door trims parted company with the doors, owners reported excessive wind noise as a result of inadequate door seals, and the interior trim of some models met with criticism. All the faults were swiftly rectified, and by the middle of 1991 the 3-series was meeting everyone's expectations: this quality, compact sedan was what every middle-manager aspired to.

Still new models kept coming, none more exciting than the M5 variant of the E34 5-series. Like its predecessor the latest M5 was subtle in its appearance, only tiny badges and 'turbine' wheels (designed to draw cooling air through the brakes) giving the game away, and then only to enthusiasts with sharp eyes. Also like its predecessor, power came from a variant of

Above: The second-generation M3 Evolution 2 shows off its sizable trunklid-mounted aerofoil.

Above: From the front the M3 Evolution 2 clearly reveals its deep front air-dam and enormous alloy wheels.

Left: Former motorcycle racer Johnny Cecotto successfully campaigned the E30 M3 and later this, the E36 320iS.

the four-valve big six engine descended from those in the racing CSLs, this time with a slightly longer stroke to expand its capacity to 3535cc. Despite the long-throw crankshaft the newest version of the multi-valve straight six was safe to 7200rpm and developed its maximum power (315bhp, 29bhp more than the old M5 despite the new car having a catalytic converter) at 6900rpm. Maximum torque was also better than before, but came at a high 4750rpm. Low-rev lugging was not what the new M5 was about, but with such awesome top-end grunt few people complained. The only criticisms were to the effect that, though massively quick, the M5 was less than entertaining – an efficient machine for covering the ground rather than a tactile pleasure for the driver, a complaint that was also commonly levelled against the 850i.

In 1991, to scotch some rumors (press speculation concerning the M8 and other models) BMW revealed a whole range of development projects which it had decided not to pursue, one of them being an M8 with a 48-valve, quad-cam V12 of around 5.4-liters. Around 500bhp propelled a machine that was lighter than a normal 8-series thanks to the use of Kevlar composite panels, so acceleration was sure to be electrifying and the top speed, assuming it was not artificially limited, would have nudged 190mph (306km/h). Other stillborn projects included a Touring station wagon version of the M3, a two-plus-two Z1, and a two-door, convertible version of the M5.

Below: As touring car regulations changed, the 318iS came to the fore. This model is competing in the Spa 24-hour race.

The M5 sedan was made even quicker two years later when the engine was enlarged yet again, to 3.8-liters, and the power peak climbed to 340bhp. It was also joined by a long-awaiting sibling, the M3 version of the E36 3-series which had been in production since 1990.

Rather different to its tearaway predecessor, this new M3 was a roadgoing machine and as a result was powered by a refined 24-valve straight-six engine rather than a revvy twin-cam four. From 3.0-liters the new engine generated 286bhp (the same as the old M5/M635CSi 3.5-liter unit) thanks to a new electro-hydraulic system called VANOS, which varied the valve timing to suit the engine speed. While a conventional engine could only have valve timing optimized for one engine speed, the VANOS system could rotate the intake cam relative to the rest of the engine to ensure that the valve timing was more effective more of the time.

Developments in another direction saw the 5-series range introduce a new element to the BMW line-up – a true station wagon. There had been a three-door version of the 2002 two decades earlier, but that was more of a hatchback than a true station wagon. There had been no attempt at a multi-role E21, but the E30 3 series had spawned a station wagon version, which was pretty but compromised by its big rear lights intruding into the tailgate aperture that made loading and unloading difficult. Though not as capacious as some of the competing quality vehicles – Volvo's station wagons were particularly cavernous – the 5-series station wagon offered an attractive blend of build quality, space, and performance. In addition to a conventional tailgate at the back, it also had a lift-up rear window for loading smaller items, which looked gimmicky but proved to be surprisingly useful. Like the 3-series station wagon and the three-door '02 before it, the new vehicle was known as a Touring.

BMW buys Rover

BMW's product line was becoming wider and more comprehensive as it strove to establish itself as a 'full line' manufacturer rather than just a purveyor of performance sedans. It was this effort which led to Munich's takeover in 1994 of the troubled British car group Rover, masterminded by BMW's new chairman, the charismatic Bernd Pischetsrieder. Rover was all that remained of the nationalized British Leyland group, which brought together some historic marques including Jaguar and Daimler, Triumph, Wolseley, Riley, Morris, and, of course, Land Rover and Rover. Leyland also included Austin, which had been the basis for BMW's first cars back in the 1920s. There was another connection, too: Anglophile Pischetsrieder was a cousin of the brilliant engineer Alec Issigonis, who had designed the million-selling Minor for Morris and the landmark Mini for Austin.

Jaguar and Daimler had been hived off some years earlier and the rest of the group, then known as Austin Rover, had been sold to British Aerospace. It entered into an agreement

Above and left: The E36 3-series was a big advance over its predecessor, with radical new styling and the new Z-axle rear suspension. Quality suffered on early cars, however, with the durability of the interior trim coming in for considerable criticism.

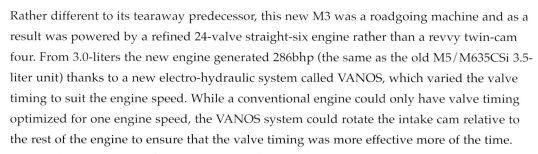

BMW 318i E36

Production	1990-92 (revised model 1993-98)
Engine	In-line six-cylinder, single overhead camshaft, 12 valves, aluminum alloy cylinder head
Bore x stroke	84mm x 81mm
Capacity	1796cc
Power	113bhp at 5500rpm
Torque	117lbft at 4250rpm
Fuel system	Bosch Motronic engine management
Gearbox	Five-speed manual, single dry-plate clutch
Chassis/body	Unitary steel chassis/body
Suspension	Front: MacPherson struts Rear: multilink and coil springs
Brakes	Hydraulically operated, discs all round
Performance	Top speed: approximately 196km/h (122mph) 0-62mph (0-100km/h): 10.0sec

BMW M3 E36

Production	1993-99
Engine	In-line six-cylinder, twin overhead camshaft, 24 valves, VANOS variable valve timing, aluminum alloy cylinder head
Bore x stroke	86mm x 85.8mm
Capacity	2990cc
Power	286bhp at 7000rpm
Torque	236lbft at 3600rpm
Fuel system	Bosch Motronic engine management
Gearbox	Five-speed manual, single dry-plate clutch
Chassis/body	Unitary steel chassis/body
Suspension	Front: MacPherson struts Rear: multilink and coil springs
Brakes	Hydraulically operated, discs all round
Performance	Top speed: approximately 155mph (250km/h) 0-60mph (0-97km/h): 5.6sec

with Honda to co-develop new models and Honda was generally seen as the ideal new owner. However, to consternation in some quarters, BMW stepped in to take control.

BMW's influence was soon felt at Rover. The British company, a mainstream car maker rather than a 'quality' producer, was seen as an ideal way for BMW to expand its market penetration. Rover's cars ranged from supermini hatchbacks like the Rover 100 (based on the old Metro) to the Honda-derived 800 executive sedan, all of them front-wheel drive. Where there was a BMW competing in the same class, the Rover was a much cheaper and more mainstream product. The idea was that BMW methods and technology would quickly be brought to bear on Rover's product development process and its manufacturing capabilities, but its products would continue to sit neatly below the BMW line-up.

The ultimate driver's car

By the mid-1990s, BMW was also involved with another British car maker, but one without the long-standing heritage of the Rover group and with considerably more glamor associated with it. As the BMW turbo era was drawing to a close, Brabham F1 designer Gordon Murray moved to McLaren, which dominated the 1988 Grand Prix season winning 15 out of the 16 races. Waiting for a plane in Italy following the one race that year that McLaren didn't win, Murray and McLaren boss Ron Dennis started discussing a roadgoing supercar project. By the end of the year the project was up and running, and by March the following year it was public knowledge. On March 12, 1990 Murray gathered together his small team and laid down the essentials for the new car in a ten-hour briefing. It was to be the ultimate driver's car, a mid-engined, three-seater design which incorporated elements which the South African designer had first conceived back in the 1960s. Compared to existing supercars the McLaren was to be exceptionally small and light (through the extensive use of carbon fiber composite materials for the structure) and would be designed to

Left: The E36 M3 Convertible provided top-down style with near-supercar performance.

Opposite: BMW expanded the 5-series range with a Touring station wagon in 1993.

maximize driver involvement – which meant no ABS, no brake servo, no traction control. It would also be amazingly powerful. Murray considered carefully the companies who could possibly supply the kind of engine he wanted – a large, normally-aspirated unit with a high output per liter – and came up with just three names: Honda, Ferrari, and BMW. Honda, then McLaren's F1 engine supplier, might have been the obvious choice but by chance Murray met Paul Rosche at the German Grand Prix in July 1990, and very quickly it was agreed that BMW would supply the engine for McLaren's new supercar.

Murray's requirements were stringent: the engine had to deliver 550bhp, yet still be light in weight (551lb/250kg or less) and small in physical size (just 24in/600mm long). It also had to be normally aspirated – Murray ruled out a turbo engine because of its non-linear throttle response – free-revving, and capable of being mounted as a stressed member, just as in a Formula 1 car. The V12 engine already used in the 7-series and 8-series was too big and too heavy for the McLaren, so Rosche promised a brand new engine which would hit every target. He was as good as his word.

Above: The 3-series quickly became the most sought-after compact executive car.

The S70/2 V12 engine which BMW Motorsport produced for the McLaren was a bespoke design which bore little resemblance to BMW's production V12. Block and heads were aluminum alloy, with Nicasil coatings for the bore surfaces to prevent wear. The pistons were forged aluminum, while the conrods and crankshaft were forged steel – all

143

McLaren F1

Production	1994-97
Engine	V12, twin overhead camshafts per bank, 48 valves, variable valve timing, aluminum alloy cylinder head
Bore x stroke	86mm x 87mm
Capacity	6064cc
Power	627bhp at 7400rpm
Torque	479lbft at 5600rpm
Fuel system	TAG engine management
Gearbox	Six-speed manual, carbon clutch
Chassis/body	Unitary carbon fiber composite chassis/body
Suspension	Double wishbones and coil springs all round
Brakes	Hydraulically operated, discs all round
Performance	Top speed: approximately 240mph (387km/h) 0-60mph (0-97km/h): 3.2sec

conventional materials for a high-performance engine. The exhaust system was a little more exotic, however, with pipework fabricated from Inconel, a heat-resistant stainless steel, and a muffler made from titanium. Dry-sump lubrication minimized the height of the engine and ensured reliable oil delivery even in fast corners and under heavy braking.

Fastest of all

BMW's VANOS variable valve timing system, already seen on the latest M3, was adapted for the V12 engine but BMW decided the extra weight and complexity of a variable geometry intake system was unnecessary. In its final specification the 6064cc engine produced no less than 627bhp at 7400rpm, with a torque peak of 479lbft (660Nm) at 5600rpm, and that meant the McLaren exceeded its performance estimates even though the car's final weight was slightly more than Murray had hoped.

The engine first ran in 'Edward,' the second of two test-bed cars built by McLaren. XP1, the first F1 prototype, was running by the end of 1992. But less than three months later, XP1 was destroyed in an accident in Namibia while BMW engineers were carrying out hot weather tests – the driver stepped out unharmed, testament to the strength of the F1's carbon fiber monocoque construction. XP2, the second prototype, then completed BMW's tests before being used for the essential crash test, which it passed with flying colors.

The McLaren project dominated the headlines, and fired the imagination of enthusiasts everywhere. This was the ultimate, no-compromise supercar, designed to be the fastest and the best with no effort to keep costs down: this was a car whose engine bay was lined with gold because that was the most effective material, whose exhaust manifolds cost more to manufacture than an entire 8-series V12 engine. BMW's awesome engine was at the heart of this, the ultimate driving machine.

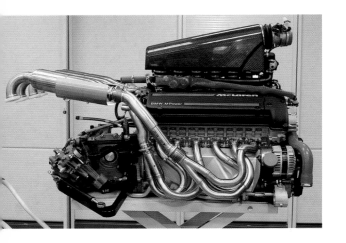

Above: BMW's S70/2 V12 engine was built specially for the McLaren F1 project. It developed over 600bhp from 6064cc.

Right: Designed purely as a road car, the three-seater McLaren would go on to have a successful racing career.

Left: The 8-series coupé sat at the top of the BMW range for a decade, from 1989 to 1999. No mere sports car, it was instead an accomplished long-distance 'Grand Touring' car.

Alpina: Building a Better BMW

BURKHARD BOVENSIEPEN began modifying BMWs in the early 1960s, producing a twin-carburetor kit for the 1500 which gave it similar performance to the 1800. In the early days Bovensiepen worked from his father's Alpina typewriter factory at Kaufbeuren, west of Munich, but by the end of the 1960s the typewriter business had been sold and the Alpina tuning company had moved up the road to Buchloe.

Along with the Schnitzer brothers, Alpina spearheaded BMW's touring car racing program around that time while the factory itself was concentrating on Formula 2. Alpina also continued to develop its road car conversions, which quickly developed a reputation not just for awesome speed but also for quality and reliability. Late in 1972 Bovensiepen's personal 3.0CSL, with around 265bhp compared to the standard 200bhp, was entrusted to a number of motoring publications, each of which returned with glowing praise: Michael Bowler at *Motor* called it a 'four-seater Dino.'

Later conversions became more ambitious, transforming Alpina into a manufacturer of cars rather than a mere tuner.

Buchloe inserted a tuned version of the 2.8-liter 'big six' engine into the E21 3-series to produce the 200bhp Alpina B6, and installed a turbocharged 3.0-liter six into the 5-series and 6-series to create the Alpina B7 models. The E28 5-series was later equipped with a normally-aspirated 3.4-liter six developing 245bhp to produce the universally acclaimed Alpina B9.

Today Alpina is still based in Buchloe and still produces parts and accessories for BMW cars and complete bespoke BMW-based performance cars for connoisseurs, ranging from the 3-series-based B3 to the 500bhp 7-series-based B7. They are machines of colossal performance but subtle appearance which are about taste and achievement rather than simply image.

Alpina B9	
Production	1972-77
Engine	In-line six-cylinder, single overhead camshaft, 12 valves, aluminum alloy cylinder head
Bore x stroke	93.4mm x 84mm
Capacity	3453cc
Power	245bhp at 5700rpm
Torque	236lbft at 4500rpm
Fuel system	Bosch Motronic engine management
Gearbox	Four-speed ZF automatic
Chassis/body	Unitary steel chassis/body
Suspension	Front: MacPherson struts Rear: semi-trailing arms and coil springs
Brakes	Hydraulically operated, discs all round
Performance	Top speed: approximately 140mph (225km/h) 0-60mph (0-97km/h): 6.8sec

Left: Alpina's distinctive multi-spoke alloy wheels have been seen on a multitude of BMWs, but the company's re-engineering of BMW designs goes much deeper.

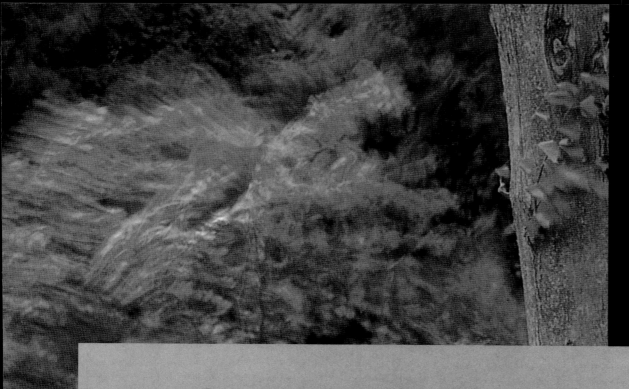

STYLE AND
SUBSTANCE
1994-99

Previous pages: BMW powered McLaren F1 GTR to its Le Mans win in 1995.

Above: The 3-series Compact was a cheaper, hatchback version of the popular sedan.

B Y THE MID-1990s BMW had completed a remarkable journey. The best-selling 'Neue Klasse' sedans of the 1960s had set them on the road to recovery, and Munich had built on its success with every succeeding generation. In the 1970s BMW had become a force in touring car racing and in Formula 2, and had been acknowledged as a maker of well-engineered sports sedans for the road. By the 1980s the 3-series had become virtually the automatic choice for every upwardly mobile executive, BMW had conquered Formula 1 with some of the most powerful engines the sport had ever seen, and Munich had built some of the fastest and most luxurious sedans in the world. Now in the early 1990s BMW dominated touring car racing once again, this time with the M3, and it was supplying an awesome, bespoke V12 engine for the McLaren F1, the fastest car in the world. It was a long way from the financially shaky days of the 1950s.

Now BMW turned its attention to making the best car in the world, the most impressive and luxurious executive sedan – a car it hoped could beat the Mercedes-Benz S-class at its own game. Munich's offering in this market during the early 1990s was the E32 7-series, replaced in 1994 by a new generation, the E38, which brought with it new styling and a new range of engines.

Car makers were now moving away from the amorphous, aerodynamic body styles of the 1980s and introducing more form into their shapes, and the new E38 7-series had sharper and better-defined lines than before. It was still clearly a BMW, and the 'twin kidney' nose was as prominent as ever, though the E38 body continued the process of reducing the height of the kidneys and increasing their width, a trend which had begun in earnest with the V12 versions of the E32.

The V12 again powered the top models in the 7-series range, but six-cylinder power of the mid-range E32s gave way to a pair of new engines. Cars were getting heavier because car buyers were taking safety more seriously again. That meant stronger construction, because equipment levels were continuing to rise, and because further improvements in refinement were being sought. Moreover, emissions regulations were getting tighter which made it harder and harder to produce a high power output, even for an engine development team as talented and experienced as BMW's. Greater engine capacity was the answer, and the old iron-block straight-sixes (closely related to the big six engines of the late 1960s) had been stretched about as far as they could go. A new straight six with space for extra capacity would have been physically longer and consequently more difficult to accommodate in the car, so instead BMW opted for a layout that it had not used since the mid-1960s – the V8.

The M60 V8 was a lightweight, all-alloy motor with twin camshafts on each bank of cylinders and four valves in each combustion chamber – by now multi-valve cylinder heads were *de rigueur* for performance engines. Unlike conventional alloy V8s these new engines

Bond's BMWs

THE 1995 James Bond film *GoldenEye* marked a series of new departures for the world's most famous secret agent. There were new producers, the film was made at a new studio, there was a new lead actor in the shape of Pierce Brosnan, and for the first time Bond's transport was provided by BMW.

British sports cars had been 007's usual preference throughout the long run of the films, predominantly Aston Martins (the DB5 in the third film, *Goldfinger*, is still Bond's best-known vehicle) and Lotuses. But for *GoldenEye* Bond was behind the wheel of a BMW Z3, before the car had even been introduced to the public. Even though its part in the film is small and the gadgets we're told it has on board are never used, the brand new BMW gained an enormous amount of exposure in the press – and Z3 sales rocketed as a result.

In 1997's *Tomorrow Never Dies*, 007 hires a 750iL at Hamburg Airport – but the Avis employee he meets is none other than equipment officer, Q, and the BMW hides a whole arsenal of weapons. Rockets in the sunroof and a tear gas dispenser are just the start, because this car can also be driven by remote control using Bond's Ericsson mobile phone. 007 uses this to escape from pursuers in a spectacular chase scene set in a multi-story car park – a sequence which was shot at the Brent Cross shopping center in London. In all, no less than 17 full-size 750iLs were used in the making of the film, and in addition scale models were built for some shots. In the same film Bond also finds himself aboard a BMW R1200 motorcycle, which leaps from roof to roof in Saigon above the spinning motor blades of a helicopter.

Bond is back in a BMW again for *The World Is Not Enough*, this time taking the wheel of a suitably modified Z8. Remote control again comes to Bond's rescue, but the Z8 meets a spectacular end when it is sliced in half by circular saw hung from a helicopter.

That was the last of the BMWs in Bond films, Bond reverting to Aston Martins for subsequent movies.

Above: Bond star Pierce Brosnan with the Z8 from The World is Not Enough.

Left: Shooting some of the driving scenes meant mounting cameras on the Z8.

BMW 320d E46

Production	1997 on
Engine	In-line four-cylinder diesel, twin overhead camshafts, 16 valves, aluminum alloy cylinder head
Bore x stroke	88mm x 84mm
Capacity	1951cc
Power	136bhp at 4000rpm
Torque	206lbft at 1750rpm
Fuel system	Common-rail direct fuel injection
Gearbox	Five-speed manual, single dry-plate clutch
Chassis/body	Unitary steel chassis/body
Suspension	Front: MacPherson struts Rear: multi-link and coil springs
Brakes	Hydraulically operated, discs all round
Performance	Top speed: approximately 128mph (206km/h) 0-62mph (0-100km/h): 9.9sec

Above right: The E46 3-series was first seen in public at the Geneva show early in 1997.

Right: E36 3-series cars were still racing in 1998: this 320d won the 24-hour production car race at the Nürburgring.

Above: Victory for the BMW V12 LMR at Le Mans. After a disappointing debut race in 1998 when the cars were withdrawn on safety grounds, the Williams-built cars came good in 1999.

Left: The winning team at Le Mans in 1999. Italian Pierluigi Martini (in the car) is flanked by Frenchman Yannick Dalmas (left) and German 'Smokin' Jo Winkelhock (right).

the hands of Yannick Dalmas, Masanori Sekiya, and J.J. Lehto. With its regulation intake restrictors the racing F1 – known as the GTR – developed only 9bhp more than the standard roadgoing car, though the talk was that, unrestricted, it was good for 800bhp. Other changes included a stripped-out interior, rose-jointed suspension, and a massive rear wing.

A roadgoing relative of the GTR, called the LM, followed in 1996. The BMW V12 was given new camshafts and a higher compression ratio, and the engine management system was remapped to liberate 668bhp. Slightly shorter gearing than standard brought the top speed down to 'only' 225mph (362km/h), but allowed McLaren to claim a 0-60mph (0-97km/h) time of less than three seconds. Only five LMs were built, all finished in the bright orange livery of Bruce McLaren's 1960s F1 team.

Long-tail McLarens

Even that wasn't the end of the F1 story, because the introduction of purpose-built sports racing machines from Porsche and Mercedes prompted McLaren to build an 'evolution' version of the F1. The F1 GT road car, of which only three were built, used the same BMW engine as before but the bodywork was now wider, lower, and longer. The 'long tail' bodywork was then applied to the racing GTRs, one of which finished fourth at Le Mans in 1997, but by now the F1 was out of its depth. Rival sports racing machines had been built specifically to get the most out of the prevailing racing regulations, rather than being designed as true road cars as the F1 had been. Production of F1 road cars ended that year, after just 100 had been built – making it one of the rarest, as well as the fastest, of all supercars.

It was a time of turmoil for sports car racing, as the administrators chopped and changed regulations in an attempt to encourage more support and more spectator interest. The

BMW V12 LMR	
Racing season 1999	
Engine	V12, twin-overhead cam per bank, 48 valves, aluminum alloy cylinder heads
Bore x stroke	86mm x 85.94mm
Capacity	5990cc
Power	590bhp (rpm n/a)
Torque	500lbft (rpm n/a)
Fuel system	Bosch engine management
Gearbox	X-Trac six-speed sequential
Chassis/body	Carbon composite body and chassis
Suspension	Front: double wishbones Rear: double wishbones
Brakes	Hydraulically operated, discs all round
Performance	Top speed: approximately 212mph (342km/h) 0-60mph (0-97km/h): approximately 4.0sec

Above: The E36 M3 convertible, like the M3 sedan, was a more refined car than its predecessor thanks to its smooth 24-valve six-cylinder engine.

'production supercar' GT1 formula had been exciting and well-supported, but now loopholes in the rules were being exploited to run what were essentially out-and-out racing machines, even if they were built for sale in tiny numbers. An alternative Le Mans Prototype class was also introduced alongside the GT cars, the Prototypes lapping faster but being hobbled with smaller fuel tanks, so they had to stop for fuel more often. It was this category which BMW chose to enter for 1998, with a car developed in conjunction with a new racing partner.

By this time Brabham was a spent force. McLaren had become the dominant team in Grand Prix racing with Honda-powered cars, but then had two variable years employing Ford and Peugeot power. During 1994 the Woking team signed with Mercedes-Benz to use its F1 engines, built in Britain by racing engine specialist Ilmor, which were already being used by Peter Sauber's Swiss F1 team. Mercedes-Benz, of course, was BMW's arch-rival, one it had been fighting one way or another since the 1930s. There could be no long-term future for McLaren and BMW while the MP4/10 and its successors carried the three-pointed star. So BMW turned to Williams, another British F1 team, to develop its new Le Mans Prototype machine – and to work toward F1 with a BMW engine. Work began on the Le Mans car late in 1997 and by April the following year the V12 LM, as the new machine was known, had run its first tests. An open-topped two-seater, the LM employed the F1's V12 engine in a 5990cc capacity, its sporting mien demonstrated by an overall weight some 440lb (200kg) less than the already light McLaren F1 road car.

Two LMs were entered at Le Mans in 1998, but the challenge ended early. After just four hours both cars were withdrawn on safety grounds when it was found that grease was escaping from the wheel bearings, and there was a consequent risk of a bearing failure.

At the time the leading BMW of Tom Kristensen, Steve Soper, and Hans Stuck had been heading the LMP1 category, while the second car of Johnny Cecotto, Pierluigi Martini, and 'Smokin' Jo Winkelhock was recovering from a collision early in the race when a Courage-Porsche spun in front of it. The new Mercedes-Benz CLK-LM failed, too, and Toyota's GT-ONE encountered tire trouble late in the race, leaving Porsche to claim victory.

Above: A new generation of 3-series cars replaced the E36 in 1998, but enthusiasts would have to wait longer for a new M3.

BMW wins Le Mans

BMW was back at Le Mans in 1999 with a revised car, now known as the LM Roadster and sporting a pair of BMW 'kidneys' at the front. This time Munich had plenty to celebrate, with Jo Winkelhock, Pierluigi Martini, and Yannick Dalmas bringing the LM Roadster home a lap ahead of its nearest competitor, the Japanese-crewed Toyota GT-ONE. Mercedes-Benz garnered all the headlines, for the wrong reasons, when its new V8-engined CLR-LM cars proved to be aerodynamically unstable and back-flipped three times over the Le Mans weekend. Eventually Stuttgart had to withdraw its cars, fortunately without serious injury to somersaulting drivers Mark Webber and Peter Dumbreck.

Away from the razzmatazz of racing, BMW had been busy building a new generation of road cars which reaffirmed Munich's ever-growing confidence. Not only were these cars faster and better-made than ever, they were wider in their scope and appeal than BMW had ever managed before. The most mainstream of these latest releases were new generations of the popular 5-series and 3-series sedan models.

The E39 5-series was announced late in 1995. Its styling followed the lead of the previous E34 5-series in its aerodynamic smoothness and incorporated more recent features from other

BMW 328i E46

Production	1997 on
Engine	In-line six-cylinder, twin overhead camshaft, 24 valves, Double VANOS variable valve timing, aluminum alloy cylinder head
Bore x stroke	84mm x 84mm
Capacity	2793cc
Power	193bhp at 5500rpm
Torque	207lbft at 3500rpm
Fuel system	Siemens MS engine management
Gearbox	Five-speed manual, single dry-plate clutch
Chassis/body	Unitary steel chassis/body
Suspension	Front: MacPherson struts Rear: multi-link and coil springs
Brakes	Hydraulically operated, discs all round
Performance	Top speed: approximately 128mph (206km/h) 0-62mph (0-100km/h): 6.6sec

Right: Strong family resemblance led the E46 to be labeled a 'mini 5-series.

Above: Like its predecessors, the E46 3-series became the most sought-after compact luxury car.

Above: BMW's driver-focused control layout was clearly in evidence in the E46 cabin.

BMW models, such as the glassed-over headlights of the 3-series. Opinion was divided over the success of the new 5-series shape, but there was almost unanimous praise for the engineering underneath. Aluminum alloy was now employed for the suspension arms and front struts, for the subframes and for the brake calipers – all of which helped save unsprung weight, which aided ride and handling, and reduce the total mass of the car to the benefit of performance and fuel economy. With a good ride, exceptional refinement, and a roomier interior than the car it supplanted, the new 5-series was well received, and with the bigger six-cylinder or sublime V8 engines installed there was talk of it being the best all-round car money could buy. As expected the sedan was soon followed by a 5-series Touring, which joined the range in 1997.

When the E46 3-series was announced at Geneva in March 1997, many people looked upon it as a 'mini 5-series' – not least because of the family resemblance at the front, where both cars had their traditional kidney grilles neatly integrated into the hood. Initially the new car was available in four-door form only, as had been the case with the previous 3-series back in 1990, and with a choice of five engines. The 318i was given a 1.9-liter four-cylinder M43 engine with twin contra-rotating balancer shafts to counteract the natural second-order vibrations of the in-line four layout. Balancer shafts were an old idea, first proposed by Frederick Lanchester before World War I, which had been enjoying a revival since the

Above: *The M Roadster used the same 321bhp six-cylinder engine as the M36 M3.*

Below: *Compared to the Z3, the M Roadster sported fatter fenders covering wider wheels.*

BMW M Roadster

Production	1997-2002
Engine	In-line six-cylinder, twin overhead camshaft, Double VANOS variable valve timing, 24 valves, aluminum alloy cylinder head
Bore x stroke	87mm x 91mm
Capacity	3246cc
Power	321bhp at 7400rpm
Torque	258lbft at 4900rpm
Fuel system	Siemens engine management
Gearbox	Five-speed manual, single dry-plate clutch
Chassis/body	Unitary steel chassis/body
Suspension	Front: MacPherson struts Rear: semi-trailing arms and coil springs
Brakes	Hydraulically operated, discs all round
Performance	Top speed: approximately 155mph (250km/h) 0-62mph (0-100km/h) : 5.3sec

1970s in car engines from Mitsubishi, Fiat, Saab, and (perhaps most notably for BMW) Porsche – the latter building four-cylinder engines of acceptable refinement despite capacities which were heading toward a full 3.0-liters. BMW's eight-valve M43 engine also had variable-length intakes which helped to boost low-speed torque without harming maximum power.

In addition to this sophisticated new four-cylinder engine, three capacities of in-line six were also available in the new 3-series, the biggest being a 2.8-liter delivering 193bhp and featuring the 'Double VANOS' system which varied the timing of both intake and exhaust valves. There was also a brand new 2.0-liter turbodiesel in the 320d, BMW's first direct injection unit. Direct injection was more fuel efficient, but tended to be noisier with a characteristic 'knock,' but that was minimized using the latest common rail injection system with two-stage injection. A variable-geometry turbocharger helped to ensure good response throughout the engine speed range, and the 136bhp generated by this 1951cc engine made it far more interesting than the four-cylinder diesel from the previous 3-series, which developed just 90bhp from its 1.7-liters. A 316i was added to the range early in 1999. Confusingly, despite the designation it was not fitted with a 1.6-liter engine. Instead, it had an 1895cc M43 engine, just like the 318i, but the latter produced 13bhp more through the use of different settings in the very sophisticated engine management system. Two-door coupé models also came on stream that year, but those who were waiting for a more exciting 3-series – an M3 – would have to be patient.

Not that BMW was slow to introduce new performance models. The four-cylinder Z3 was soon joined by a 2.8-liter six-cylinder version, and then in 1997 BMW unveiled an altogether more serious M-car version. The M Roadster had the old-shape E36 M3's engine under its nose, a 3.2-liter, 24-valve straight-six with no less than 321bhp, and the same underpinnings also went into a curious three-door hard-top version called the M Coupé. Shattering acceleration delivered 0-60mph (0-97km/h) from rest in a fraction over five seconds in either car, and they rocketed up to their electronically-limited top speed of 155mph (250km/h).

Above left: The M Roadster's interior was swathed in leather. The car's performance was electrifying.

Above: Like the M Roadster, the M Coupé made use of the 3.2-liter M3 engine.

Below: The M Coupé was just as fast as the Roadster, though there were dark comments criticizing its 'bread van' rear styling from some quarters.

Much the same headline figures were on offer from the E39 M5 which appeared in 1998, though it was a very different car in most other respects. For the first time the M5 was powered by a V8 engine, descended from the 4.4-liter M62 V8 in the latest 540 (a mildly updated version of the troublesome M60 V8 that had debuted in the E34 5-series and E38 7-series). Motorsport's S62 version was a much-modified 4941cc engine which developed nearly 400bhp, in part due to the VANOS variable valve timing on all four camshafts. Control of the engine was through a 'drive by wire' throttle pedal, which sent electrical signals to the engine management system rather than mechanically controlling the engine's throttle butterflies. A 'Sport' button on the dash allowed the driver to select a different response curve for the pedal, making the engine feel lively even with gentle pedal pressure, and at the same time reduced the assistance given by the Servotronic power steering to allow a greater degree of feedback.

In addition to ABS and traction control, BMW included a system called Dynamic Stability Control which automatically throttled back the engine and, if necessary, applied the brakes on one or more wheels to keep the car on line in high-speed corners. The M5 retained the

Left: The third-generation M5 departed from the six-cylinder engines of previous models – instead it had a 4.9-liter V8 producing almost 400bhp.

Below left: Clear instrumentation, always a BMW forte, conveyed a wealth of information to the M5 driver.

BMW M5 E39

Production	1998-2002
Engine	V8, twin overhead cams per bank, 32 valves, alloy block and heads
Bore x stroke	94mm x 89mm
Capacity	4941cc
Power	394bhp at 6600rpm
Torque	369lbft at 3800rpm
Fuel system	Siemens engine management
Gearbox	Six-speed manual or SMG sequential gearbox
Chassis/body	Unitary steel chassis/body
Suspension	Front: MacPherson struts Rear: multi-link and coil springs
Brakes	Hydraulically operated, discs all round
Performance	Top speed: 155mph (250km/h) 0-60mph (0-97km/h): 5.3sec

aluminum suspension of the regular 5-series, and as with previous generations it looked little different to lesser models in the range – though the drainpipe dimensions of the four exhaust tailpipes were a clue to the M5's awesome output. Quicker than any previous M5, the latest car was also more refined and more usable, more than ever a genuinely practical and luxurious everyday sedan that just happened to be every bit as fast as a Ferrari.

Ferrari customers would, no doubt, have countered that their car had the edge over the M5 in the styling department, but when BMW unveiled the Z8 in 1999 Maranello's clients might have had less to shout about. The big 8-series coupé, which ended its run the same year, had been a mile-munching GT car, but the Z8 had quite a different character. It was nothing less than a full-blown supercar, which matched colossal performance with drop-dead gorgeous looks and extreme exclusivity.

BMW Z8	
Production	1999-2003
Engine	V8, twin overhead cams per bank, 32 valves, alloy block and heads
Bore x stroke	94mm x 89mm
Capacity	4941cc
Power	394bhp at 6600rpm
Torque	369lbft at 3800rpm
Fuel system	Siemens engine management
Gearbox	Six-speed manual or SMG sequential gearbox
Chassis/body	Aluminum spaceframe and outer panels
Suspension	Front: MacPherson struts Rear: multi-link and coil springs
Brakes	Hydraulically operated, discs all round
Performance	Top speed: 155mph (250km/h) 0-60mph (0-97km/h): 4.7sec

Inspired by the 507

Like the Z3 before it, the Z8 drew its inspiration from the 507 of the late 1950s. Danish designer Henrik Fisker had styled it in America, at BMW's new design studio in California, and the car had been unveiled in concept form in 1997. The vehicle which reached production two years later was similar, but lacked the concept car's Jaguar D-Type/Mercedes SLR head fairings on the rear deck – instead there were twin roll hoops behind the seats. The nose and the side-vents were clearly inspired by the BMW 507, while there was a hint of 1960s Austin-Healey about the crease along the sides at door handle height. Intriguingly, a couple of years earlier rumors had surfaced in Britain that BMW chairman Bernd Pischetsrieder, a classic car enthusiast, intended to revive the long-dead Austin-Healey name, though nothing ever came of it.

The styling may have had a retro feel about it, but there was nothing old fashioned about the engineering. Powering the Z8 was the 400bhp V8 engine from the M5, and the Z8 was even quicker than that luxurious sedan thanks to its lighter weight. The spaceframe structure underlying the Z8, its stressed outer panels and the suspension components were all aluminum alloy, gave the Z8 a 298lb (135kg) weight advantage over the M5. The result was a 0-60mph (0-97km/h) sprint time of around 4.7 seconds, fast enough to worry a Ferrari 550 or the Aston Martin Vanquish (another Fisker design). Like the products of those famous marques, the Z8 was hand-made in small numbers for a select clientele.

As if the latest M5 and the new Z8 and the prospect of a new M3 were not enough, BMW fans could now look forward to the return of the blue and white roundel to the hallowed world of Formula 1 motor racing. One of Paul Rosche's last jobs before his retirement had been to work his magic on a new Grand Prix engine, this time a 3.5-liter normally-aspirated V10, which made its first runs during 1999. In 2000 it would power the new BMW-Williams F1 car – and Munich was out to win.

Left: Z8 styling details, such as the horizontal front grilles and the vents in the front fenders, were inspired by the 1950s 507.

Opposite below: The Z8 was a full-blown supercar, deriving huge performance from the V8 engine it shared with the M5 sedan.

Below: BMW's first US factory, at Spartanburg in South Carolina. It now builds the Z4 roadster and X5 SAV.

Spartanburg: BMW builds in America

AS WELL as widening its range during the 1990s, BMW began to turn itself into a global player, rather than soley a German manufacturer. BMWs had been assembled in South Africa for many years to avoid the high taxes imposed on imported cars, but now BMW spread its wings wider. The buyout of Rover took BMW into Britain, where the company would eventually remodel the old Morris factory at Cowley to become the production plant for its Mini, and a new engine plant would be established at Hams Hall in the Midlands.

As far back as June 1993 BMW announced plans to build a new manufacturing plant at Spartanburg in South Carolina, alongside Interstate 85. Work began in September that year, and within a year the production lines were being set up. The first American-made BMW, a 318i, rolled off the line on September 8, 1994.

In addition to supplying cars for the home market, Spartanburg became the home of Z3 production which began in September 1995. The M Roadster was added to the line-up in January 1997, and later that year Spartanburg celebrated production of the 100,000th roadster. M Coupé production began in January 1998, and in May work began on an extension to accommodate production lines for the new X5 4x4. Such was the success of the roadsters and the X5 that further expansion was announced in June 2000, and there was a double celebration early in 2001 – with the production of the 50,000th X5 and the 250,000th roadster.

Today Spartanburg continues to build the X5 models in their thousands, and since 2002 it has produced the Z4 roadster. Every summer many of those cars return to South Carolina as Z3 and Z4 fans gather for the 'Roadster Homecoming.'

GENERATION
X
1999-2004

Previous pages: BMW re-entered Formula 1 with Williams, its Le Mans partner. This is Ralf Schumacher at Imola in 2001.

BMW X5

Production	1999 on
Engine	V8, twin overhead camshafts per bank, 24 valves, aluminum alloy cylinder heads
Bore x stroke	92mm x 82.7mm
Capacity	4398cc
Power	282bhp at 5400rpm
Torque	325lbft at 3600rpm
Fuel system	Siemens engine management
Gearbox	Six-speed automatic
Chassis/body	Unitary steel chassis/body
Suspension	Front: MacPherson struts Rear: multi-link and coil springs
Brakes	Hydraulically operated, discs all round
Performance	Top speed: 130mph (209km/h) 0-62mph (0-100km/h): 7.0sec

Right: The V12 Le Mans car engine was shoe-horned into an experimental X5. It was capable of 192mph (309km/h).

Opposite: The X5 'sports activity vehicle' astounded critics with its on-road ability and performance.

A FAD FOR four-wheel-drive performance cars swept through the European motor industry in the 1980s, fueled by the arrival of the all-drive Audi quattro in 1980. Though the time of the four-wheel-drive performance car quickly passed, sedans and station wagons with four driven wheels – rather than cumbersome off-roaders – continued to be popular in some parts of Europe and the US. All-weather ability was the key to their appeal, and they became particular favorites with German and Austrian skiing enthusiasts. BMW entered the arena with four-wheel-drive versions of the 3-series and 5-series from 1985, known as the 325iX and 525iX, using the sophisticated Ferguson transmission system. This incorporated a viscous coupling which automatically locked when one axle spun faster than the other, improving traction in poor conditions.

Four-wheel drive enjoyed a revival in popularity in the 1990s when proper 4x4s – known in the US as 'Sports Utility Vehicles' or SUVs – started to shake off their utilitarian roots and develop into machines that were both affordable and usable on the road. Until then the only 4x4 that had been capable off the road and also pleasant to drive on it had been the Range Rover (which became part of BMW's portfolio in 1994). As other 4x4s caught up, suddenly the SUV became a vehicle people aspired to, and sales rocketed.

A BMW SUV could not simply be a utilitarian 4x4 station wagon, and especially not one with truck-like construction. Accordingly when the X5, as the new machine was called, was unveiled at the Detroit Motor Show in 1999 it proved to be a far more sophisticated machine, based around a car-like monocoque structure. Munich spent a lot of time and effort honing its handling and grip to the point where it could match a conventional road car despite its weight and the inevitably high center of gravity dictated by the upright body.

The result was a new yardstick by which the on-road ability of SUVs was assessed – so much so that BMW liked to put the X5 in a class of its own, calling it a 'Sports Activity Vehicle' or SAV. Performance was also exceptional for the class, early models being fitted with the alloy 4.4-liter V8 from the 5-series – giving the X5 a 130mph (209km/h) top speed and vivid acceleration. Styling was another strong suit, the X5 cleverly blending the tough, chunky looks of off-road vehicles with traditional BMW styling cues. The American

engine built in partnership with Chrysler powered it, giving the entry-level Mini One 90bhp and the sportier Mini Cooper 115bhp. At the Tokyo show later in 2001 a supercharged Cooper S was announced, boasting 163bhp from its 1.6-liters.

The flame-surface idea got its second public airing in 2003 with the announcement of a new 5-series. Wider use of aluminum made this fifth generation 5-series lighter than the old car, and like the 7-series it benefited from the latest Double VANOS V8 engines and common rail diesels, plus 2.0-liter and 2.5-liter gasoline sixes. In addition to the electronic systems which had already been seen on the 7-series, the new Five could be ordered with Active Steering, a system which dynamically altered the steering ratio and assistance depending on circumstances – steering effort was reduced during maneuvering while at the same time the steering was made more direct, while at high speeds the gearing and assistance were lower to improve stability and feel. The interior was dominated by a second-generation iDrive system, and even featured air conditioning which maintained humidity, avoiding the drying effect of conventional systems. The flame-surfaced exterior was, according to BMW, 'muscular,' 'bold,' and 'dramatic' – though elsewhere opinion was still divided.

The other flame-surface BMW, the 7-series, had already been boosted by the introduction of long-wheelbase versions, and in 2003 the range expanded still further. BMW added a pair

Above: Long-wheelbase versions of the 7-series were introduced in 2002. The extra length went into the rear cabin, providing ample legroom.

Above: The 6-series coupé was added to the range in 2003. This convertible version followed, the first BMW in its class since the 1950s.

173

Mini Cooper S

Production	2002 on
Engine	In-line four-cylinder, transversely mounted, single overhead camshaft, 16 valves, aluminum alloy cylinder head
Bore x stroke	77mm x 85.8mm
Capacity	1598cc
Power	163bhp at 6000rpm
Torque	155lbft at 4000rpm
Fuel system	Siemens engine management
Gearbox	Six-speed manual, single dry-plate clutch
Chassis/body	Unitary steel chassis/body
Suspension	Front: MacPherson struts Rear: multi-link and coil springs
Brakes	Hydraulically operated, discs all round
Performance	Top speed: approximately 135mph (217km/h) 0-60mph (0-97km/h): 7.4sec

Inset: Even the 'basic' Mini One with 90bhp was fun to drive. All the Minis are built at the former Rover factory at Cowley near Oxford.

Right: BMW's recreation of the Mini concentrated on quality, looks, and driver appeal. The Cooper S could be identified by the intercooler air intake in the hood.

BMW Z4 3.0

Production	2002 on
Engine	In-line six-cylinder, twin overhead camshafts, 24 valves, Double VANOS variable valve timing, aluminum alloy cylinder head
Bore x stroke	84mm x 89.6mm
Capacity	2979cc
Power	231bhp at 5900rpm
Torque	221lbft at 3500rpm
Fuel system	Siemens engine management
Gearbox	Six-speed manual or automatic
Chassis/body	Unitary steel chassis/body
Suspension	Front: MacPherson struts Rear: multi-link and coil springs
Brakes	Hydraulically operated, discs all round, ABS
Performance	Top speed: approximately 155mph (250km/h) 0-62mph (0-100km/h): 5.9sec

of diesels to the range, a six-cylinder 3.0-liter and a 4.0-liter V8 – though some markets, such as the UK, got only the smaller of the two oil-burners. Both offered gasoline-engine levels of refinement, together with good economy and plenty of low-end torque.

At the top of the range, deliveries began of the 760i and long-wheelbase 760Li, featuring a new 6.0-liter V12 motor crammed with BMW's latest engine technology. Valvetronic variable valve lift and direct injection, plus Double VANOS variable valve timing, helped the V12 to deliver impressive fuel economy despite a prodigious outputs of up to 408bhp and 442lbft. High Security versions were also introduced that year, featuring an integrated double layer of steel armor. The High Security cars had protection built in during production (carried out at Dingolfing) ensuring that areas such as the pillars were well-protected – unlike other security vehicles, which had their armor retro-fitted after the vehicle was built, potentially leading to areas of weakness. In tests by German authorities the car proved it could withstand attack from explosives and 7.62mm-caliber weapons, winning a 'B6/B7' rating, the highest available. The High Security 7-series was used by government officials and high-ranking industrialists in the West, the Middle East, and the former Soviet Union, offering much the same internal comforts as the regular 7-series models and similar performance, though top speed was down to 130mph (210km/h).

An armored 3-series was also available, the 330i Security being intended to prevent theft, robbery, or car-jacking, as a result of which it was designed to withstand attack from a .44 Magnum revolver. The E46 3-series soldiered on as one of the dwindling number of 'old school' BMWs, the cars that had been introduced before the flame-surface Chris Bangle era. The long-awaited M3 version turned out to be a 343bhp projectile which introduced a new 'variable M differential lock' which optimized traction on challenging road surfaces. A short run of even quicker, lightweight M3 CSL cars was built during 2003, with a 234lb (110kg) weight advantage over the regular M3 through the use of carbon fiber for some interior and exterior panels and deletion of the air conditioning system and radio (though they were still available as no-cost options). Modifications to the engine's breathing system boosted the CSL's power output to 360bhp.

The 6-series coupé which followed later in the year marked a return to the mid-range coupé market which had been vacated when the 8-series was introduced, and it was a more successful implementation of the flame-surface idea than the 5-series and 7-series had been. BMW made much of the styling lines flowing around the car to harmonize front and rear. 'The curved surfaces emanate a feeling of power and breed pure emotion, creating an aura of visual tension not allowing even the slightest touch of boredom. This is not just the design of an outstanding coupé, but also an expression of unique, aesthetic character,' said Munich's rather breathless press release. The new 6-series certainly exuded style, and like most recent BMW cars it introduced a new group of innovative options. A head-up display projected important data directly into the driver's line of vision, while BMW's Adaptive Headlights automatically swivelled as necessary in response to steering angle, yaw rate, and vehicle speed.

Z4 to the fore

Another warm reception greeted the Z4 roadster, the flame-surfaced replacement for the 007-endorsed Z3. Here the sharp-creased styling was in its element, making the Z4 a distinctive

Above and opposite: The Z4 was the most successful example yet of Chris Bangle's 'flame surfacing' styling ideas.

Below: Performance was a Z4 strength, and an M-badged version may yet appear.

Rover and out

BMW's takeover of Rover, championed by BMW chairman Bernd Pischetsrieder, had been intended to turn BMW into a 'full line' manufacturer, giving it a finger in every automotive pie. Rover's lower-priced range would fit neatly under BMW's premium products, allowing the Munich empire to expand into a wider marketplace without devaluing the BMW brand itself.

But for all the ballyhoo and optimism surrounding the takeover in 1994, BMW's ownership of the British company lasted just six years, during which sales slumped and losses mounted. Despite investment in new product and modernization of production plants, BMW still couldn't turn the ailing Rover Group into a profit maker. The 'English Patient' weakened its parent company to the point that VW and Ford were rumored to be thinking of takeover bids for BMW.

The last straw proved to be the launch of the mid-range Rover 75 in 1998. Pischetsrieder chose that moment to hint that the Longbridge factory still wasn't safe from closure – and suddenly the big story was the threat to Longbridge rather than Rover's new car. Worse, BMW was forced to delay production by six months due to the appalling quality of the cars, and when they finally did come on

stream, the 75s simply didn't sell the way they needed to.

In 2000 Munich admitted defeat, and new chairman Joachim Milberg sold Land Rover, the only part of the group which had credible products and a promising future, to the Ford Motor Company. There it became part of Ford's Premier Automotive Group alongside Jaguar, Aston Martin, Volvo, and Lincoln – under the control of none other than Wolfgang Reitzle, who had left BMW after disagreements with the board over Rover.

BMW retained the Mini brand and the new Mini which was shortly to enter production at the Cowley plant, now called BMW Oxford. Venture capitalists Alchemy Partners expressed interest in the rest, but in the end it was a group of businessmen (several of them ex-Rover, including former boss John Towers) who took control in May 2000. BMW wrote off Rover's debts, and Phoenix bought the stricken company – which represented so many of Britain's mainstream car makers – for just £10.

Above right: BMW's Mini amid the yellow cabs of New York city. This is the convertible.

Right: Tiny British sports car maker Morgan turned to BMW to power its new Aero 8.

and refreshing new entry into the roadster market – which, of course, had always been as much about style as it had been about performance. Not that the Z4 was lacking in speed, either, equipped as it was with a choice of 2.5-liter and 3.0-liter straight-six engines with up to 231bhp. Later a 2.2-liter six was added to the line-up and an entry-level model with a 2.0-liter four-cylinder engine would join the range to expand the Z4's affordability. Alpina filled the gap for those wanting more peformance with a 300bhp, 3.3-liter version of the Z4 known as the Roadster S.

The Z4 was the first BMW to use electric, rather than hydraulic, power steering – a move which improved fuel consumption (unlike hydraulic assistance it used no power at the straight-ahead position) and also allowed greater flexibility in the way assistance was provided. A 'Dynamic Drive Control' button reduced assistance to give the driver more feedback, at the same time sharpening-up the throttle response and changing the gear-change point if the car was fitted with an automatic or sequential manual transmission. Another innovation was the use of PAX runflat tires, which would spread to other BMWs in time. Though the PAX tires delivered a harsher ride than conventional rubber, there was no argument about the safety and convenience benefits they brought.

Arguably even greater style, if a little less in the way of electronic equipment, was being supplied by Morgan, the tiny British sports car company based in Malvern, in the English Midlands. After years of relying on the evergreen Rover V8 engine for its fastest model, the Plus 8, Morgan had decided it was time to move on to a more powerful and more modern power unit. Renowned for the old-fashioned styling of its cars, the company had always kept abreast of engine developments, and for its latest Aero 8 model – developed out of its GT racing machines – Morgan turned to BMW. Munich's engineers helped to incorporate the 4.4-liter M62 V8 engine and a six-speed Getrag gearbox into the aluminum-chassised Morgan, giving it 286bhp and the potential for very modern supercar performance. A five-

BMW M3 CSL	
Production	2003
Engine	In-line six-cylinder, twin overhead camshafts, 24 valves, Double VANOS variable valve timing, aluminum alloy cylinder head
Bore x stroke	97mm x 91mm
Capacity	3246cc
Power	360bhp at 7900rpm
Torque	273lbft at 4900rpm
Fuel system	Siemens engine management
Gearbox	Paddle-shift SMG six-speed gearbox
Chassis/body	Unitary steel chassis/body
Suspension	Front: MacPherson struts Rear: multi-link and coil springs
Brakes	Hydraulically operated, discs all round, ABS
Performance	Top speed: 155mph (250km/h) 0-62mph (0-100km/h): 4.9sec

Above: Modifications to the M3 engine boosted power to 360bhp for the CSL version.

Left: Deleting the air conditioning system and radio, and using carbon fiber for some components, gave the M3 CSL a small weight advantage over the standard car.

179

Above: BMW-Williams driver Juan Pablo Montoya fought McLaren's Kimi Räikkonen and Ferrari's Michael Schumacher for the World Championship in 2003.

second 0-60mph (0-97km/h) sprint time was easily achievable, and despite a shape that still wasn't all that slippery (though far better than previous Morgans), the Aero 8 still broke the 160mph (257km/h) barrier.

F1 with Williams

Even quicker were the BMW-powered products of another British car maker – the Formula 1 team Williams. The Oxfordshire team had struggled since the heady Renault-powered days of 1996 and 1997 when Damon Hill and Jacques Villeneuve had won them successive world titles. Renault had pulled out of F1 in 1997 but privately prepared versions of its engines continued to power the Williams cars, under the Mecachrome and Supertec names, in 1998 and 1999. The BMW/Williams partnership which had won Le Mans now moved on to F1, Williams' heartland, and BMW's E41-4 V10 engine first ran in a Williams chassis in April 1999 before making its Grand Prix debut the following season. The drivers were Ralf Schumacher and the young Briton Jenson Button, who had just one season to prove himself before the arrival at Williams of former Champ Car driver Juan Pablo Montoya for 2001.

Schumacher Junior finished third in the BMW-Williams cars' first Grand Prix, in Australia. It didn't take long for the BMW engines to earn a reputation as the most powerful in the sport, even if their reliability was less than perfect – and for the team's drivers to show off their undoubted talents. In Brazil Montoya used his Champ Car experience to out-fumble Michael Schumacher's Ferrari as the field re-started following a Safety Car period, then led

High Rollers: BMW's battle for the best car in the world

Rolls-Royce and Bentley cars were built in the same factory in Crewe, Cheshire, until 2003. When parent company Vickers decided to sell in 1997, BMW, already an engine supplier to Rolls-Royce/Bentley, put in an offer but a month later VW announced its own bid, plus a plan to buy Cosworth Technology from Vickers. By July 1998 an agreement was reached for VW to take over the Crewe factory and build Rolls-Royce and Bentley cars until 2003, when BMW would take over the Rolls-Royce brand.

BMW considered several sites for its new Rolls-Royce factory. From the start it was decided that Rolls-Royce should stay in Britain, and the location had to have good transport links, easy access to a test track and proximity to a skilled workforce. BMW also wanted a location in an attractive part of the country, as it expected many Rolls-Royce customers to visit the factory. Eventually it was decided to build the new headquarters and manufacturing plant at Goodwood in Sussex, near to the famous race track.

By June 2002 BMW had built its first Rolls-Royce car, called the Phantom. New from the ground up, the Phantom had an aluminum space frame body and a purpose built 6.75-liter V12 engine developing 453bhp and 531lbft of torque, effortlessly propelling the new Rolls-Royce to 149mph (240km/h) and to 60mph (97km/h) from rest in just 5.7 seconds. Rear-hinged 'coach doors' provided easy access to the back seat, and the car was crammed with clever detailing – from the retractable Spirit of Ecstasy figurehead at the front to the 'RR' logos on the wheels which always remained upright. With a price tag of over 320,000 Euros ($425,000) the Phantom remains BMW's most expensive, and most exclusive car.

Rolls-Royce Phantom	
Production	2003 on
Engine	V12, twin overhead camshafts per bank, 48 valves,
Bore x stroke	84.6mm x 92mm
Capacity	6749cc
Power	453bhp at 5350rpm
Torque	531lbft at 3500rpm
Fuel system	Direct fuel injection
Gearbox	Six-speed ZF automatic
Chassis/body	Aluminum alloy space frame and outer panels
Suspension	Front: wishbones and air springs Rear: multi-link and air springs
Brakes	Hydraulically operated, discs all round, ABS
Performance	Top speed: 149mph (240km/h) 0-60mph (0-97km/h): 5.7sec

the race until his BMW-Williams was assaulted from behind by Jos Verstappen's Arrows. At Imola, Ralf Schumacher won the team its first race and there were more good results that year. The 2002 season got off to the wrong kind of flying start when Ralf's Williams climbed over the back of Rubens Barrichello's Ferrari in Australia, but later in the season the BMW engine proved its performance and Montoya proved his class with a string of pole positions. In 2003 Montoya joined Kimi Räikkonen and Michael Schumacher in a three-way battle for the World Championship, eventually resolved in Schumacher's favor. With improved reliability and class-leading power the BMW-Williams drivers became regular F1 front runners – and BMW once again challenged for a World Championship.

Above left: BMW took over the Rolls-Royce brand in 2003 and built a new factory at Goodwood to produce the new Phantom.

TODAY AND TOMORROW
2004 AND BEYOND

Previous pages: BMW released the first official pictures of the new 3-series late in 2004.

BMW-Williams FW26

Racing season	2004
Engine	BMW P83 V10, 40 pneumatic valves, aluminum block and cylinder heads
Bore x stroke	Not revealed – approximately 89mm x 48mm
Capacity	2998cc
Power	Not revealed – approximately 900bhp at 18,500rpm
Torque	Not revealed – approximately 295lbft at 16,000rpm
Fuel system	BMW management system
Gearbox	Seven-speed semi-automatic
Chassis/body	Carbon-Aramid-Epoxy composite
Suspension	Front: Double wishbones Rear: Double wishbones
Brakes	Carbon discs and pads, AP calipers
Performance	Top speed: approximately 224mph (360km/h)* 0-62mph (0-100km/h): 2.5sec* 0-124mph (0-200km/h): 4.5sec*

* Depending on gearing, which varies between circuits

Right: Colombian Juan Pablo Montoya challenged for the championship in 2003.

AFTER THE BMW-Williams F1 team's successful 2003, when it was second in the constructors' championship and Juan Pablo Montoya challenged hard for the drivers' title, the 2004 season proved to be frustrating. The FW26 sported a new nose with curving, wide-based struts carrying the wing, quickly dubbed the 'walrus nose', which was intended to clean up the airflow under the car. Power came from a new V10 engine, the P83, which like other modern F1 engines used pneumatic valves – but unlike some competing engines it could spin to well over 19,000rpm and develop more than 900bhp.

Michael Schumacher's Ferrari dominated the early part of the season, then tangled with Montoya in the Monaco tunnel while the field was running under the Safety Car. By mid-season Schumacher Senior was setting up a record-breaking winning run, and Sam Michael had taken over from Patrick Head as Technical Director of Williams. Both Williams cars were disqualified from the Canadian Grand Prix in June when their brake cooling ducts were judged to be illegal. Sam Michael accepted the decision but pointed out that the inlet area was no bigger than was allowable, and hence there had been no gain in performance.

Worse still, at Indianapolis Ralf hit the wall hard, an accident that meant he missed much of the second half of the season – his place being taken in turn by Williams test driver Marc Gené, and former Jaguar driver Antonio Pizzonia. Montoya, meanwhile, was disqualified again, this time for illegally swapping to the spare car after his race car developed problems on the Indianapolis grid.

By the time of the Hungarian GP in August Williams had returned to a more conventional front-end for its cars and it had become clear that both Williams drivers were on their way to other teams for 2005, Ralf departing for Cologne-based Toyota and Juan Pablo leaving for McLaren-Mercedes. Jaguar's Australian driver Mark Webber was signed up for one Williams seat, and then Jenson Button astonished the F1 world by announcing he would be returning to Williams to fill the other. Button's 2004 team BAR battled to keep its star driver, claiming it had a valid contract with Button for 2005. When F1's Contracts Recognition Board agreed with BAR, Button's move was put on hold, leaving Webber as

undisputed team leader at BMW-Williams. When Button ultimately does join the team it will set up a strong driver line-up – and Williams' policy of letting its drivers race each other harder than many other teams would set up some fascinating on-track battles.

Above: Ralf Schumacher in the 'walrus nose' BMW-Williams FW26 at Albert Park, Melbourne in 2004.

Formula BMW

More future F1 front-runners were being schooled in the action-packed Formula BMW single-seater series – including Bruno Senna, nephew of the great Ayrton Senna. The cars resembled mini-F1 machines, with wings and racing tires, their front wing supports designed to look like BMW grille 'kidneys.' All the Formula BMW machines were powered by 140bhp BMW motorcycle engines, the cars' even performance leading to some great racing. There were four Formula BMW championships – in Asia, Germany, the UK, and the USA – each supporting one or more F1 races during its season.

BMW-Williams: F1's power brokers

Frank Williams began racing as a driver, but soon switched to team management, running Brabham F2 and F1 cars in 1968/9 and de Tomaso F1 cars in 1970. The Williams team switched to March, then to its own Len Bailey-designed car which ran as a Politoys and an Iso-Marlboro. Williams teamed up with Walter Wolf for 1976 to run Heskeths, then fielded March cars in 1977 before again producing its own cars, designed by Patrick Head. The team's first Grand Prix victory came at the British GP in 1979, and Australian driver Alan Jones drove the FW07B to win the World Championship in 1980. Williams won the constructors' title that year

and again in 1981, then Keke Rosberg won a second drivers' title for the team in 1982.

Early in 1986 a road accident while driving back from a test session in France left team boss Frank Williams paralysed. His team used Honda V6 turbo engines to win its third constructors' title that year, but drivers Nelson Piquet and Nigel Mansell took points off each other allowing McLaren's Alain Prost to win the drivers' championship. Piquet and Williams won the world titles in 1987, but outclassed Judd engines were the best Williams could secure for 1988. A switch to Renault made Williams winners again, securing both world titles in 1992 (with Nigel

Mansell) and again in 1993 (Alan Prost). Ayrton Senna joined the team for 1994 only to lose his life in a crash at Imola, but Damon Hill rallied the team and helped win a seventh Constructors' Cup. Hill won the drivers' title in 1996 and team-mate Villeneuve won in 1997, Williams winning a further two constructors' championships.

After engineering BMW's 1999 Le Mans win, Williams brought BMW engines into F1 in 2000 and immediately the team's prospects looked up. Juan Pablo Montoya challenged for the championship in 2003, and few would bet against Williams being one of Ferrari's stiffest rivals in years to come.

Above: BMW-Williams in 2004. From left: Patrick Head (Technical Director and later Director of Engineering), driver Juan Pablo Montoya, test driver Marc Gené, BMW engine man Mario Theissen, driver Ralf Schumacher, and team boss Sir Frank Williams.

Munich's road car range carried its own hopes for the future, thanks to some additions to established ranges and some completely new models. In July 2004 the year-old 6-series range, initially powered by V8 engines only, was enlarged with a brand new straight-six becoming available. BMW pointed to its aluminum/magnesium composite construction and claimed it was the world's lightest six-cylinder, a 3.0-liter unit with Valvetronic technology developing 258bhp at 6600rpm, 12 percent more than BMW's existing 3.0-liter six. It was enough to give the 630i spritely performance, but still allowed it to deliver impressive fuel economy figures. A convertible version of the 6-series was also now available, returning BMW to the touring convertible sector which had not seen a Munich machine since the demise of the V8-engined 503 Cabriolet in 1959.

Left: *Formula BMW was powered by a 140bhp BMW motorcycle engine.*

Formula-BMW FB2

Racing season	2004
Engine	In-line four-cylinder, twin overhead camshaft, 16 valves, aluminum alloy cylinder head
Bore x stroke	70.5mm x 75mm
Capacity	1171cc
Power	140bhp at 9250rpm
Torque	86lbft at 6850rpm
Fuel system	Bosch Motronic engine management
Gearbox	Hewland six-speed sequential gearbox, single dry-plate clutch
Chassis/body	Carbon/Kevlar composite monocoque with aluminum honeycomb insert
Suspension	Front: Double wishbone Rear: Double wishbone
Brakes	Hydraulically operated, discs all round
Performance	Top speed: approximately 143mph (230km/h) 0-62mph (0-100km/h): approximately 5.0sec

The new M5 was more familiar territory, though the latest generation looked very different to the previous one and was powered by a very different engine. The in-line sixes of the first M5s back in the mid-'80s had given way to a 32-valve V8 and now to a 5.0-liter V10, the first engine of this layout to go into a BMW production car. The V10 revved to 8250rpm and delivered up to 507bhp, which was channeled through a seven-speed sequential manual gearbox which incorporated a 'launch control' function to maximize acceleration from rest. The 3869lb (1755kg) M5 could dispatch the benchmark 0-62mph (0-100km/h) sprint in just 4.7 seconds and power on to 124mph (200km/h) in 15 seconds, and there was enough urge to propel the new M5 to 205mph (330km/h) – though, as ever, it was electronically limited to 155mph (250km/h). BMW claimed the new M5 could lap the challenging Nürburgring Nordschleife in a very rapid eight minutes.

Astonishing though the latest M5's performance was, its styling was perhaps even more significant. Once again BMW's radical flame surfacing was to the fore, but there was evidence of further improvement in the execution of this controversial style 'language.' This addition to the 5-series range was not only by far the fastest, it was also the best-looking example yet.

Expanding the range

Also adding to the 5-series range was a new Touring, which combined all the benefits of the sedan with an even more practical load space than previous Touring generations. An optional powered tailgate made loading and unloading easier: all you had to do was push a button on the remote control and the tailgate would magically swing into action, while the

BMW 116i

Production	2004 on
Engine	In-line four-cylinder, twin overhead camshaft, 16 valves, aluminum alloy cylinder head
Bore x stroke	84mm x 72mm
Capacity	1596cc
Power	115bhp at 6000rpm
Torque	111lbft at 4300rpm
Fuel system	Siemens engine management
Gearbox	Five-speed manual, single dry-plate clutch
Chassis/body	Unitary steel chassis/body
Suspension	Front: MacPherson struts Rear: multi-link and coil springs
Brakes	Hydraulically operated, discs all round
Performance	Top speed: approximately 125mph (201km/h) 0-62mph (0-100km/h): 10.8sec

load space cover would automatically retract out of the way. As before the rear window could be opened independently for loading small items. The load area itself was bigger than the previous Touring, and with the optional runflat tires fitted there was no need to carry a spare wheel – further increasing the space available for luggage. At launch the Tourings were available with a choice of two gasoline engines (the 2.5-liter six and 4.4-liter V8) and two diesels (2.5-liter and 3.0-liter straight-sixes).

BMW's range of new Minis expanded to include the supercharged Cooper S and diesel-engined One D. Early in 2004 Convertible versions of the Mini One and Cooper were added, each boasting a powered roof and a drop-down tailgate reminiscent of the original Mini 45 years earlier. By August, production of Minis had reached the half-million mark. Not content with this assault on the supermini market, BMW then pressed ahead with a compact hatchback to slot in below the 3-series in the main Munich range.

This was the 1-series, which took BMW into a hotly-contested market for premium hatches against upmarket models from Alfa Romeo, Audi, Ford, Opel/Vauxhall, Seat, Volkswagen and many others. All these machines took the usual small-hatch engineering route with front-wheel-drive and transverse engines, but BMW's new offering was different. The 1-series retained the classic front engine/rear-wheel drive layout, compromising interior space slightly but delivering better traction, better steering feel, and more entertaining handling than any other car in its class. BMW had toyed with front-wheel drive in the mid-1990s, building a front-drive 3-series Compact prototype, but after Munich's acquisition of the Rover Group in 1994 its own front-drive cars had become surplus to requirements. Now Rover was history, BMW had decided to concentrate on premium products, and the dynamic benefits of rear-wheel drive outweighed the packaging difficulties.

Even the entry-level 1-series, the 116i, boasted a 115bhp 1.6-liter engine with Double VANOS variable valve timing, and buyers prepared to spend a bit more could choose from a 150bhp 120i, or a pair of common-rail diesel engines – the 120d being the quickest of the initial 1-series cars. More engine choices followed, and more body styles are likely. The 1-series will probably sire coupé, convertible, and notchback sedan models which will be sold under the 2-series moniker. The convertible has already been seen in concept form, dubbed the CS1, at the 2002 Geneva show exhibit which first gave us a taste of the 1-series shape.

A new 3-series, the E90, follows in 2005. Previous 3-series ranges have encompassed several different body styles – two-door Coupé, three-door Compact, four-door sedan, five-door Touring – but it seems likely that the next 3-series will be available only as a four-door

Opposite above: The 1-series moved BMW into a market segment that it had not occupied since the 1960s.

Opposite below: A Touring station wagon was added to the 5-series range in 2003. As ever the car blended luxury, refinement, and performance with space and versatility.

Below: The latest M5 is powered by a 507bhp V10 engine, and will lap the Nürburgring in eight minutes.

BMW M5

Production	2004 on
Engine	V10, twin overhead cams per bank, 40 valves, Double VANOS variable valve timing, aluminum alloy cylinder heads
Bore x stroke	92mm x 75.2mm
Capacity	4999cc
Power	507bhp at 7750rpm
Torque	384lbft at 6100rpm
Fuel system	BMW M engine management
Gearbox	Seven-speed sequential gearbox
Chassis/body	Unitary steel chassis/body
Suspension	Front: MacPherson struts Rear: multi-link and coil springs
Brakes	Hydraulically operated, discs all round
Performance	Top speed: 155mph (250km/h) 0-62mph (0-100km/h): 4.7sec

sedan or five-door station wagon, with sportier two-door models badged as the 4-series. But what of BMW beyond 2005?

We can get some clues from the concept cars which have graced BMW's motor show stands in recent years. While some have given us an early look at production models which would soon follow – like the Z07, which became the Z8, the X coupé which previewed the Z4's shape and the CS1 which was a good clue to the 1-series – others have been tantalizing glimpses of ideas and technology which might one day form part of BMW's growing range of cars.

Some have promised to take BMW into market sectors from which it is currently absent. The Z9 GT car of 1999, for instance, indicated that at some time in the not too distant future BMW might consider producing a modern 8-series, a flagship coupé with refinement and class to go along with awesome speed, with the latest electronic wizardry assisting the driver and maximizing safety.

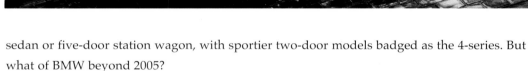

Showcasing the future

Other concepts, like the X coupé and the xActivity cars, have shown that future BMW models might start to blur the lines between the traditional sectors: X coupé was a sporting two-door based on the four-wheel-drive chassis of the X5, giving it go-anywhere appeal but without sacrificing the sense of style and fun that a coupé brings. The xActivity show car was almost the opposite, starting with the station wagon-like body of a 4x4 (the still-secret X3) and turning it into an airy 'frame structure convertible.' Other manufacturers have also released concept cars which start to blend together the virtues of different types of vehicle, and if this cross-pollination of ideas begins to win public acceptance then it is certain that we will see some exciting new multi-role vehicles emerge from Munich.

BMW's manufacturing plants around the world will play an increasingly important role, too, as the tiny German car maker that once struggled to find its feet in the turbulent financial climate of the 1920s becomes more and more a global giant of the motor industry in the 21st century. The hiccup of the controversial 'flame surfaced' styling will be forgotten as BMW develops the style into something more palatable, and as buyers get used to these challenging new shapes. Meanwhile modern BMWs will continue to cast backward glances at their forebears. The kidney grille has been around in a variety of forms since the 1930s while the 'Hofmeister kink' in the C-pillar, created by BMW design chief Wilhelm Hofmeister for the Neue Klasse sedans in the early 1960s, continues to feature on Munich's cars to this day.

Meanwhile the quality of BMW's engineering, which has never been in much doubt, continues to shine through all its products and makes them ever more popular. That strength in engineering powers BMW's performances in motor sport, too, with success in every arena – in touring car racing, at Le Mans, and in arguably the pinnacle of the sport, Formula 1. There will be plenty more success, on track and off it, and the cars bearing the blue and white roundel are sure to be winners for many years to come.

Opposite far left: *BMW's 'iDrive' system was intended to reduce the complexity of a modern luxury car's dashboard, but it met with a mixed reaction.*

Opposite: *BMW's concept cars are often direct pointers to future production models. The Z07 concept became the Z8 roadster.*

Opposite below: *Do the Z9 coupé and cabrio concepts reveal future plans for a range-topping GT car? Only time will tell.*

Below: *BMW's hydrogen-powered H2R set nine world records in a single day at the Miramas Proving Ground in September 2004. Using an adapted version of the 760i's 6.0-liter V12, the H2R proved capable of 187mph (300km/h). BMW have been developing hydrogen car technology since 1978, and a production hydrogen-powered 7-series isn't far away.*

Index